Key Stage Three

Shakespeare

The Tempest

This book is for 11-14 year olds.

It's packed with all the really important stuff you need to know about *The Tempest* if you want to do well in your Key Stage Three SAT Shakespeare Question.

We've stuck loads of pictures and jokes in to make it more fun — so you'll actually use it.

Simple as that.

PROSPERO →

The TEMPEST

a play by William Shakespeare
presented in Multicolour

IN THE MIDDLE OF THE MEDITERRANEAN SEA... NOT FAR FROM MY MAGIC ISLAND...

ARIEL →

MY LITTLE GIRL MIRANDA'S WATCHING FROM SHORE...

Oh no – those poor people. I hope they won't drown.

MIRANDA

BACK ON BOARD...

We're going to sink. Let's swim for it!

There's an idea...

SEBASTIAN — Alonso's brother

ALONSO — King of Naples

FERDINAND — Alonso's son

ANTONIO — Duke of Milan, and Prospero's brother

GONZALO — a nice old man

STEPHANO — a butler

TRINCULO — a jester

MIRANDA COMES TO SEE ME AT THE BEACH HUT...

Did you start this storm, dad?

Yes – and I'll tell you why. It all started many years ago...

Believe it or not I used to be Duke of Milan, but I was into books and magic, not politics...

ALONSO

ANTONIO

My brother Antonio and the scheming King of Naples hatched a plot to get rid of me...

They threw you and me out of Milan and set us adrift on the open sea in a leaky old boat... Luckily, good old Gonzalo put my books of magic on the boat.

It's pure chance we didn't drown. We ended up on this island.

There was nobody here, apart from that idiot-monster Caliban...

...good old Ariel...

...and a load of other magical spirits.

So now do you see why I started the storm? All my enemies are on that ship. They won't drown but I'm going to teach them a lesson.

Contents

SECTION 5 — WRITING AN ESSAY

SECTION 6 — TYPES OF QUESTION

SECTION 7 — THE SET SCENES

Published by Coordination Group Publications Ltd.

Contributors:
Taissa Csàky
Charley Darbishire
Katherine Reed
Edward Robinson
Elisabeth Sanderson
Gerry Spatharis
Jennifer Underwood
Nicola Woodfin

With thanks to Keri Barrow, Paula Barnett and Rachel Selway for the proofreading.

ISBN: 978 1 84146 485 5

Groovy website: www.cgpbooks.co.uk

Jolly bits of clipart from CorelDRAW®
Printed by Elanders Hindson Ltd, Newcastle upon Tyne.

Preparing Your Answer

Preparation is the key to doing well in your exam. So, before you start writing, plan what you're going to write. This will make everything a lot easier, even if it sounds like loads of extra work.

You Have to Know the Set Scenes Really Well

1) The Shakespeare paper tests how well you know the play.
2) It's all about the set scenes. These are printed in full in Section 7 of this book.
3) You have to know these scenes like the back of your hand.

Learn your set scenes... or the puppy gets it.

You'll know which bits of the play you have to write about before the exam — which means you won't get any nasty surprises on the day. As long as you've learnt 'em, that is.

Take Time to Plan Your Answers

Planning might seem like a waste of precious exam time. But if you just start writing without planning you'll end up spouting rubbish. Planning makes your answer loads better.

1) Read the question carefully. It's based on the set scenes, so your answer needs to cover both these scenes.

e.g. Act 1 Scene 2 and Act 4 Scene 1
How does Prospero feel about the possible marriage of Miranda and Ferdinand in these scenes?

For this question, you need to write first about Prospero's feelings in Act 1 Scene 2, then how his feelings have changed in Act 4 Scene 1.

2) Read through the scenes again. Look for anything the characters say that will help you answer the question. When you find something useful, underline it. E.g. For the question above you would look for anything that Prospero says about Ferdinand or Miranda.

3) Next, think about what the main points of your essay will be. Make a list.

e.g.
• how Prospero feels about Miranda
• Prospero's feelings about Ferdinand
• how Prospero and Miranda have been treated in the past
• why Prospero decides to make things difficult for the couple
• what Prospero learns from "testing" Ferdinand

Do you see my point?

4) Include all your main points in the essay. Then you'll be on your way to a good mark.

Preparation, that's what you need...

You'll feel a lot more relaxed once you've got a good plan to fall back on. Once that's sorted you can focus on each point one at a time. This makes the whole exam thing a lot less scary.

Writing Well and Giving Examples

Examiners are a funny lot, but it's easy enough to <u>impress</u> them if you know what makes them tick. Here's a few <u>useful little tricks</u> that'll have them <u>gasping in admiration</u>.

Use Examples to Show You Know Your Stuff

It's crucial that you use <u>examples</u>. They show <u>evidence</u> of the points you're making. As my old granny used to say, "An opinion without an example is like a boy-band without a rubbish dance routine." Or something.

<u>Quotes</u> are really useful examples. Examiners love 'em. Remember to:

I couldn't unlock the key scenes.

1) Start and end quotes with <u>speech marks</u>.
2) Copy out the words <u>exactly</u> as they are in the play.
3) Explain <u>why the quote is a good example</u> — what does it tell you?

Sort Out Your Writing

1) Sound <u>enthusiastic</u> about the play. Use plenty of <u>adjectives</u> (describing words).

> The atmosphere in this scene is exciting and magical — Shakespeare makes Prospero appear impressive through the combination of his powerful language and mysterious spells.

2) Check your <u>spelling</u> and <u>punctuation</u>. Otherwise the examiner might not know what you mean.
3) Write in <u>paragraphs</u>. A page that's full of writing with no breaks is <u>tough to read</u>. Remember, <u>a new topic = a new paragraph</u>.

Write About Versions of the Play You've Seen

If you've seen a <u>film</u> or <u>theatre</u> version of the play, you can write about that too — <u>as long as it relates to the question</u>.

This is another good way of sounding <u>interested</u> in the play. Just make sure you mention <u>which version</u> of the play you saw.

Keep in mind that each version can be very <u>different</u>. The <u>costumes</u>, <u>settings</u> and <u>personalities</u> of the characters can all vary.

> In the 2004 film version of the play, the director, Ivor Megaphone, shows the magic in this scene by using colourful visual effects and making Prospero's voice echo strangely.

I'll make an exam-ple of you...

Exams aren't really that complicated. They ask you a <u>question</u>, you <u>answer</u> it. If you're <u>prepared</u>, there'll be no nasty surprises. <u>Stick to the point</u>, and there's nowt to worry about.

Stage Directions, Acts and Scenes

It's really important that you know what <u>stage directions</u>, <u>acts</u> and <u>scenes</u> are. Acts and scenes are like the <u>skeleton</u> of the play, and stage directions tell you what's going on <u>on-stage</u>.

Stage Directions Tell You Who's Doing What

<u>Stage directions</u> tell the actors what to do, e.g. <u>when to come on stage</u> and <u>when to go off</u>. They sometimes say <u>who</u> they have to talk to as well. They're usually written in <u>italics</u> or put in <u>brackets</u>:

The <u>names</u> of the characters are written here to tell you who's <u>speaking</u>.

PROSPERO [*to Ariel*]   Thou shalt be as free
As mountain winds — but then exactly do
All points of my command.
ARIEL   To th' syllable.
PROSPERO [*to Ferdinand*]
Come, follow. [*to Miranda*] Speak not for him.
                Exeunt.
Act 1, Scene 2, 501-504

This stage direction shows <u>who</u> Prospero is <u>speaking to</u>.

<u>Exeunt</u> means more than one person <u>leaves</u> the stage.

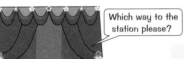
Which way to the station please?

The <u>line numbers</u> often <u>vary</u> in different printed versions of the play — so <u>don't worry</u> if these line numbers don't exactly match your copy.

Remember, plays are supposed to be <u>performed</u>, not read. So <u>stage directions</u> are really helpful for imagining how the play would look <u>on-stage</u>.

Acts and Scenes Split Up the Play

1) The play is divided up into <u>five</u> big chunks called <u>acts</u>. Each act tells us <u>part</u> of the story. Put them all together and you get the <u>whole</u> story.

2) Acts are also divided up into even <u>smaller</u> chunks called <u>scenes</u>. Scenes <u>break up</u> the story. A <u>new</u> scene might be in a different <u>place</u>, at a different <u>time</u>, or with different <u>characters</u>.

Are you sure this is the right scene?

E.g. The first scene of the play is set on a <u>ship</u> during a <u>storm</u>. The next scene happens on an <u>island</u> nearby, then the third takes place a bit <u>later on</u>, on a <u>different part</u> of the island.

Stop it, you're making a scene...

<u>Acts</u> and <u>scenes</u> are actually <u>really handy</u>, as they can help you <u>find</u> the speech or bit of action you're looking for. Remember — the play has <u>5 acts</u> and <u>loads of scenes</u>.

The Tempest as a Play

Check out these tips and you'll really get to grips with the play.

It's a Play, Not a Novel

It's meant to be acted, not just read. When you read the play, it's hard to imagine what it will look like on stage. Try and see the characters in your mind. Think about:

- what kind of people they are
- how you think they would say their lines
- how they would act

If you want some idea of how the play might look when it's acted out, you could watch it on video or DVD. Your school might have a copy of it — it's worth asking. Just remember: each version will be different.

Sometimes Characters Talk to Themselves

1) In real life, this is odd. In plays, it's normal — it doesn't mean they've gone bananas.

2) The characters talk to themselves to let the audience know what they are thinking and how they are feeling.

3) When someone talks to themself on an empty stage, it's called a soliloquy (or monologue).

4) If someone talks to the audience when there are other people on stage, it'll say [Aside] by their name in the play. The audience can hear what is being said, but the other characters can't.

The Tempest is a Comedy

Shakespeare wrote three main kinds of play: tragedies, comedies and histories. The Tempest is a comedy, but that doesn't mean the whole thing is meant to be funny. Much of it is fairly light-hearted though, and all Shakespeare's comedies have a happy ending.

Most of the funny bits are the scenes with Stephano, Trinculo and Caliban. They spend most of their time being drunk and coming up with silly schemes.

These scenes might not seem side-splitting to you or me, but Shakespeare's audience would have been roaring with laughter...

She's temper than he is, but I'm the Tempest...

If you're not used to reading plays, it's bound to feel odd at first. The fact that the play was written ages ago, and the characters are noblemen and weird creatures, takes some getting used to.

Odd Language

Some of this <u>old language</u> is hard to get your head round. But once you get the hang of <u>reading it</u> things will become a lot <u>clearer</u>. Just remember these <u>rules</u>:

Don't Stop Reading at the End of a Line

1) Follow the <u>punctuation</u> — read to the <u>end of the sentence</u>, not the end of the <u>line</u>.

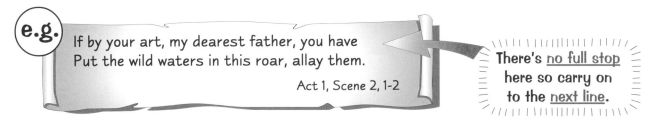

e.g. If by your art, my dearest father, you have
Put the wild waters in this roar, allay them.

Act 1, Scene 2, 1-2

There's <u>no full stop</u> here so carry on to the <u>next line</u>.

2) These <u>two lines</u> actually make up <u>one sentence</u>:

If by your art, my dearest father, you have put the wild waters in this roar, allay them.

3) Most lines start with a <u>capital letter</u> — but this doesn't always mean it's a <u>new sentence</u>.

4) <u>Full stops</u>, <u>question marks</u> and <u>exclamation marks</u> show you where the sentence ends.

Sometimes You Have to Switch the Words Around

1) Shakespeare likes to <u>mess around</u> with the <u>order</u> of words. It helps him fit the sentences into the <u>poetry</u> (see page 7).

2) If a piece of writing looks like it's <u>back-to-front</u> — <u>don't panic</u>.

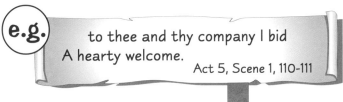

e.g. to thee and thy company I bid
A hearty welcome.

Act 5, Scene 1, 110-111

3) <u>Play around</u> with the <u>word order</u> and it'll <u>make sense</u>. What this <u>really</u> says is:

I bid a hearty welcome to thee and thy company.

Sense make doesn't Shakespeare...

I know Shakespeare's language looks really <u>different</u> from the English we speak, but it's actually <u>pretty similar</u>. Once you've got the <u>word order</u> sorted you're well on the way to <u>sussing it out</u>.

More Odd Language

Shakespeare was around over <u>400 years ago</u> — so the language he uses can seem a bit <u>weird</u>. Some of the words are <u>old words</u> that we <u>don't use any more</u>.

Thou, Thee and Thy Come Up a Lot

Once you know what these words mean, things get <u>a lot easier</u>. Happy days.

Thou = you

Thee = you

Thy = your

Thou liest, most ignorant monster.
Act 3, Scene 2, 24

I'll manacle thy neck and feet together.
Act 1, Scene 2, 464

I thought to have told thee of it
Act 4 Scene 1, 168

Verbs Can Look Odd

Hast thou seen the size of this carrot?

Often, the difference is just a couple of <u>extra letters</u> on the end of the verb. Take off the <u>t</u> or <u>st</u> and you'll see what they mean.

e.g.

hath, hast = has	wilt = will	doth, dost = does
didst = did	thinkst = think	speakst = speak

These verbs often go with <u>thou</u>, like this:

Say again, where didst thou leave these varlets?
Act 4, Scene 1, 170

Some Words are Squashed Together

The word <u>it</u> often gets <u>stuck to the next word</u>, and <u>loses the "i"</u>.

'Tis an outrage!

e.g.
'twas = it was   'twere = it were
'tis = it is   is't = is it

An i for an i...

<u>Dropping letters</u> from words isn't that strange when you think about it. We still do it in modern English, like when we change <u>it is</u> to <u>it's</u>. Shakespeare just drops <u>different letters</u>.

Poetry

There's lots of <u>poetry</u> in Shakespeare's plays. If you understand the poetry, it'll <u>help you understand</u> some of the reasons behind the <u>strange language</u>.

How to Spot Poetry

<u>Prose</u> means writing that <u>isn't poetry</u>.
There's a lot of <u>poetry</u> in The Tempest — and <u>here's how to spot it</u>:

> ### Poetry has:
>
> 1) Capital letters at the start of each line
> 2) 10, 11 or 12 syllables in each line

A <u>syllable</u> is a unit of sound. The word <u>poetry</u> has 3 syllables – <u>po</u> <u>e</u> <u>try</u>.

Poetry Doesn't Have to Rhyme

1) Some poetry <u>rhymes</u>, some <u>doesn't</u>.

e.g.

> You nymphs, called Naiads, of the windring brooks
> With your sedged crowns and ever-harmless looks
> Leave your crisp channels, and on this green land
> Answer your summons. Juno does command.
>
> Act 4, Scene 1, 128-131

Each line starts with a <u>capital letter</u>.

e.g.

> Here in this island we arrived, and here
> Have I, thy schoolmaster, made thee more profit
> Than other princes can that have more time
> For vainer hours, and tutors not so careful.
>
> Act 1, Scene 2, 172-175

This bit of poetry is in <u>rhyming couplets</u> — the first line rhymes with the second, and the third rhymes with the fourth.

This <u>doesn't rhyme</u> — but it's <u>still poetry</u>.

2) The language sometimes sounds <u>strange</u> because Shakespeare tries to get <u>each line</u> to contain the <u>right amount of syllables</u>.

3) Most of The Tempest is written in poetry — although some of the <u>less posh</u> characters, like Caliban and Trinculo, talk in <u>prose</u> (speech that isn't poetry).

You did ask for three silly bulls?

Leann Rimes — with what?

Once you realise you're dealing with <u>poetry</u>, it becomes much easier to work out <u>what it means</u>. And the rules for <u>spotting it</u> are pretty simple — just remember that it doesn't have to rhyme.

Revision Summary

Right, let's see how much you know about Bill Shakespeare and his odd little ways. If you haven't read any of Shakespeare's stuff before, it's easy to be flummoxed by the way he writes. But trust me, the more you read, the easier it gets. If you get stuck on any of these questions, look back through the section to find the answers. Then have another go, without looking back.

1) What's the point of stage directions?

2) What does "exeunt" mean?

3) What's the play split up into?

    a) Chapters and verses   b) Nooks and crannies   c) Acts and scenes

4) A play is meant to be:

    a) ignored   b) burnt   c) performed

5) What is a soliloquy?

6) If it says "Aside" by a character's name, who can hear what they're saying?

    a) The other characters   b) The audience   c) Belgians

7) The Tempest is a:

    a) tragedy   b) comedy   c) docu-soap

8) "A new line of poetry means it's a new sentence." True or false?

9) If a piece of writing doesn't make sense, what should you do?

    a) Change the word order   b) Phone a friend   c) Cry

10) When was Shakespeare around?

    a) 400 years ago   b) 200 years ago   c) 65 million years ago

11) What do these words mean?

    a) Thou   b) Hath   c) Didst   d) 'Twas

12) What does each line of poetry start with?

13) How many syllables are there in a line of poetry?

14) Does all poetry rhyme?

Am I the only one struggling with the lingo?

Who's Who in the Play

Some of the characters in this play are good and some are very bad. And not all of them are human...

Prospero — the true Duke of Milan

Prospero was betrayed in the past — he lost his title and has had to live on the island ever since. He has magical powers and uses them to put things right.

PROSPERO

Alonso — King of Naples

Alonso was involved in the plot to betray Prospero and cast him adrift with Miranda, years ago. In the end he feels sorry for what he did.

ALONSO

Miranda and Ferdinand — the young lovers

Miranda is Prospero's daughter and she grew up on the island. Ferdinand is Alonso's son, and he's a prince. These two fall in love at first sight.

MIRANDA

FERDINAND

Caliban — a savage monster

Caliban's mother was a witch called Sycorax. Caliban's always lived on the island. He's badly behaved and Prospero uses him as a slave.

CALIBAN

Ariel — a flying spirit

In the past, Prospero saved Ariel from imprisonment. Now Ariel has to be Prospero's servant, until he can earn his freedom.

ARIEL

Antonio and Sebastian

Antonio is Prospero's brother. Sebastian is Alonso's brother. Antonio betrayed Prospero and had him banished. He tries to get Sebastian to kill Alonso so they can both have more power.

ANTONIO

SEBASTIAN

Stephano and Trinculo — Alonso's servants

Stephano is Alonso's butler — he's drunk most of the time. Trinculo is Alonso's jester. They're both pretty greedy. They plot with Caliban to kill Prospero.

STEPHANO

TRINCULO

Gonzalo — an honest old man

He's good-hearted and tries to help out. He packed food, drink and books in Prospero's boat when he and Miranda were set adrift. He also tries to cheer Alonso up.

GONZALO

Some Lords, Sailors and Spirits

The Master and the Boatswain run the ship. Adrian and Francisco are a pair of Lords. There are also some strange spirits who perform a play for Prospero.

ADRIAN

FRANCISCO

MASTER

BOATSWAIN

Prospero

Prospero is at the centre of all the action and he's the <u>most powerful</u> character in the play. He <u>controls</u> the other characters and events — he's like a director and main character rolled into one.

Prospero's a Master of Magic

1) Prospero's <u>magic powers</u> are pretty extraordinary. With Ariel's help, he causes the <u>storm</u> that shipwrecks everyone on his island. He can <u>cast spells</u> that keep people exactly where he wants them.

2) He has power over <u>spirits</u>. He calls them up to lay on a <u>trick banquet</u> for Alonso and his followers. He calls them up again to perform a <u>masque</u> (a weird play) when Ferdinand and Miranda get engaged.

3) He's <u>intelligent</u> and <u>determined</u>. He's gained his powers through years of <u>studying</u> books of magic.

And after the masque, I've rented the DVD of "Castaway"...

Cool.

Ooh I love Tom Hanks.

Everyone Knows He's In Charge

1) Prospero's <u>tough with Caliban</u>. He'll <u>torture</u> him if he has to and Caliban knows it. He keeps Caliban as his <u>slave</u>, and gives him <u>painful punishments</u> if he disobeys.

2) He's <u>strict with Ariel</u> too — even though he treats him fairly most of the time. There's no question — Ariel has to <u>do as he's told</u> or Prospero will never set him free.

3) It's part of Prospero's <u>plan</u> for Ferdinand to marry Miranda. He doesn't make it easy though. He <u>tests Ferdinand</u> by keeping him prisoner and making him work hard. When Miranda and Ferdinand are engaged, he warns him pretty severely that he's <u>not to sleep with Miranda</u> before the wedding.

> Sour-eyed disdain, and discord, shall bestrew
> The union of your bed with weeds so loathly
> That you shall hate it both. Therefore take heed,
> Act 4, Scene 1, 20-22

He Can be Generous, Wise and Forgiving

1) He's a <u>good father</u> to Miranda. It's obvious he loves her. He <u>protects</u> her and arranges for her <u>happy future</u>.

2) Antonio and Alonso have <u>plotted against him</u>. So do Stephano, Trinculo and Caliban. He could take <u>revenge</u> on them all — but he decides to <u>forgive</u> them. He says that he will <u>reward Gonzalo</u> for his loyalty too.

3) He <u>keeps his promise</u> to free Ariel, even though he'll miss him.

Like David Blaine — but good at magic...

Prospero's <u>not</u> as straightforward as he might at first appear. Yes he's a kind, forgiving bloke most of the time, but he's certainly <u>no pushover</u>. Just look at the way he keeps Caliban and Ariel in line.

Ariel

Shakespeare described Ariel as "an airy spirit". He <u>makes things happen</u> all over the island.

Ariel Owes His Freedom to Prospero

1) A witch called Sycorax <u>imprisoned</u> Ariel in a tree on the island for 12 years. Prospero <u>freed</u> Ariel with his magic. Ariel then became Prospero's <u>servant</u>.

2) Ariel is keen to do what Prospero commands so that he can <u>earn his freedom</u>. He keeps pointing out what a <u>good job</u> he's doing. He doesn't want Prospero to forget his promise to let him go.

> Remember I have done thee worthy service,
> Told thee no lies, made thee no mistakings, served
> Without or grudge or grumblings.
> Act 1, Scene 2, 248-250

He Makes Sure Prospero's Plans are Carried Out

1) On Prospero's instructions, Ariel <u>creates the storm</u> that brings King Alonso and his court to the island. At the end of the play it's Ariel's job to arrange <u>calm weather</u> for the journey back to Italy.

2) He can <u>fly</u> and become <u>invisible</u>. This is how he <u>overhears</u> Caliban plotting with Stephano and Trinculo to kill Prospero.

3) He can use <u>music</u> to help Prospero's plans along — he uses songs to <u>lead Ferdinand to Miranda</u>, and another of his songs <u>wakes up Gonzalo</u> to stop Antonio and Sebastian from killing Alonso. He charms Caliban, Stephano and Trinculo with music and leads them into a stinking <u>pond</u>.

You are beautiful, In every single way...

I say, what an annoying song. I'd better follow it...

4) Ariel can <u>change his shape</u> too. He helps Prospero set up a feast for Alonso, Sebastian and Antonio, then he appears as a <u>harpy</u> (a bird-like monster) and makes the food <u>disappear</u>. Ariel also appears as the goddess <u>Ceres</u> in the masque.

He is Rewarded for His Service

1) Ariel longs to be <u>completely free</u>. Prospero promises Ariel that he will let him go if Ariel helps him <u>carry out his plans</u> on the island.

2) At the end of the play Prospero says he'll miss him — but he <u>keeps his word</u> and sets him free.

Guaranteed to give you whiter whites...

Ariel's <u>vital</u> in making Prospero's plans work. He <u>serves Prospero</u> throughout the play and Prospero eventually rewards him by setting him <u>free</u>. In this way he's the <u>opposite</u> of Caliban (see p.15), who had his freedom before Prospero arrived on the island but is now Prospero's slave.

Alonso and Gonzalo

Alonso is <u>King of Naples</u>. Gonzalo is a nice old <u>lord</u>. Gonzalo sticks with Alonso and <u>helps him out</u>.

Alonso Has Done Wrong — and He Knows it

1) Alonso is an old <u>enemy of Prospero</u>. He allowed <u>Antonio</u> to betray Prospero and take over as Duke of Milan. He was persuaded by the promise of more <u>power</u> and <u>money</u>. He didn't stop the plan to cast Prospero and Miranda adrift in a <u>rotten boat</u> either — even though he <u>knew</u> they would probably <u>die</u>.

2) He's really <u>sad</u> on the island because he thinks his son, Ferdinand, <u>drowned</u> in the storm. Alonso wears himself out looking for him, and this at least shows how much he <u>loves his son</u>.

3) After Ariel accuses him of his crimes, he <u>feels bad</u>. He thinks he's being <u>punished</u> for his sins and says he'll die looking for Ferdinand.

You've been a very naughty King.

Oh I know...(sob)

it did bass my trespass.
Therefore my son i'th'ooze is bedded, and
I'll seek him deeper than e'er plummet sounded,
And with him there lie mudded.
Act 3, Scene 3, 99-102

4) His experiences have taught him a <u>lesson</u>. At the end of the play he asks Prospero and Miranda to <u>forgive</u> him. He's <u>delighted</u> about Ferdinand and Miranda's engagement and promises to be a <u>second father</u> to Miranda.

Gonzalo is Loyal and Optimistic

He hadn't even packed any clean pants...

1) Gonzalo thought it was <u>unfair</u> when Antonio had Prospero and Miranda set adrift in a boat. Gonzalo packed <u>food</u>, <u>water</u>, <u>clothes</u> and <u>books</u> for them. It helped them <u>survive</u>. The books helped Prospero study and gain his <u>magic powers</u>.

2) He's <u>calm</u> and looks on the <u>bright side</u>. He says they were <u>lucky</u> to survive the shipwreck. He thinks the island is <u>beautiful</u>. He's <u>thrilled</u> when he finds out that Miranda and Ferdinand are going to marry.

Now, good angels preserve the King!
Act 2, Scene 1, 306

3) He's very loyal to Alonso — he tries to <u>cheer him up</u> when he's worried about Ferdinand. When Ariel wakes Gonzalo up his first thoughts are for his <u>king's safety</u>.

4) He is <u>innocent</u> and <u>honest</u>. That's why he <u>can't hear</u> Ariel accusing the others of wickedness. Prospero knows Gonzalo's a <u>good man</u> — he calls him a "noble friend".

Not to be confused with Gonzo from the Muppets...

Although Alonso was a bit of a cad in the past, he vows to <u>mend his ways</u> in the end. Gonzalo was good to Prospero in the past, and now he's good to Alonso — he's just an all round <u>diamond geezer</u>.

Antonio and Sebastian

Antonio and Sebastian are a pair of nasty villains. They plot to kill Alonso, and have no regrets.

Antonio is Dangerous and Ambitious

1) Antonio is Prospero's brother. In the past, Prospero loved and trusted Antonio — big mistake. With Alonso's help, Antonio betrayed Prospero, took over as Duke of Milan and had Prospero and Miranda set adrift at sea. He seems to have no sense of right and wrong, and scoffs at the idea of having a conscience.

2) He's a bad influence on Sebastian. Antonio persuades Sebastian to help him kill Alonso by pointing out that Sebastian would then become King. He knows he won't win Gonzalo over — so they plan to kill him too.

> Twenty consciences
> That stand 'twixt me and Milan, candied be they
> And melt, ere they molest!
> Act 2, Scene 1, 277-279

I've got a great idea...

What is it? Tell me tell me tell me.

3) He can be quite witty — but in a nasty sort of way. He makes fun out of Gonzalo, with Sebastian joining in. He's got no sympathy for Alonso either.

4) Ariel accuses Antonio of his crimes but this doesn't make him ashamed. Even when Prospero forgives him at the end of the play — and calls him "unnatural" — it doesn't seem to make him feel guilty for what he's done.

Sebastian is Selfish and Easily Led

1) Sebastian is Alonso's brother — but he doesn't feel sorry for him when he sees him grieving for Ferdinand. He even tells him that it was his own fault. He says that the shipwreck would never have happened if Alonso hadn't travelled to his daughter's wedding in Africa.

2) He's very easily persuaded to plot against his brother Alonso. He's tempted by the power of becoming King. He's very quick to make up a lie when Gonzalo wakes up and catches him with his sword drawn.

3) Sebastian doesn't feel sorry for anything he's done — just like Antonio. After Ariel accuses him he gets quite aggressive. He decides to go after the spirits to fight them.

> But one fiend at a time,
> I'll fight their legions o'er.
> Act 3, Scene 3, 102-103

Concentrate on their good points — er... um...

These two are just plain bad. Their evil plan fails, but they're not sorry they tried. Makes you wonder why Prospero forgives them really — although he does have some harsh words for them.

Ferdinand and Miranda

Miranda and Ferdinand are a <u>perfect match</u>. Things are tricky for them at first though.

Ferdinand is a Dashing Young Man

1) Ferdinand is <u>King Alonso's son</u>. He thinks his father drowned in the storm and he's very <u>upset</u> — he doesn't care about being King himself. He's chuffed when he realises his father is alive.

2) He's <u>good looking</u>. Miranda calls him "A thing divine" and <u>falls in love</u> with him straight away.

Next, you must paint the entire island purple.

Okie doke.

3) He's <u>brave</u> and <u>strong</u>. Francisco says he was seen <u>swimming strongly</u> through the stormy waves. He carries out all the <u>difficult tasks</u> Prospero sets him and puts up with being his prisoner. This shows he's <u>mentally tough</u> too.

4) Ferdinand is a typical <u>romantic figure</u>. He's a <u>noble prince</u> and his love is powerful and deep. Prospero makes him <u>earn the right</u> to marry Miranda. He passes the test.

5) He's <u>not annoyed</u> at Prospero for the way he treated him — he calls him a "second father". His engagement to Miranda brings Alonso and Prospero <u>closer together</u> at the end.

Miranda is Pure and Innocent

1) She's been on the <u>island</u> since she was a <u>little child</u>. Prospero brought her up and taught her to be obedient and kind. She's <u>beautiful</u> too.

2) She's <u>shocked</u> when Prospero tells her the story of their journey from Milan to the island. She's <u>good-hearted</u> and worries that she would have been a <u>burden</u> to Prospero — but he says she gave him the <u>will to go on</u>.

3) She's <u>upset</u> by the way Prospero <u>tests Ferdinand</u>. She says she's never seen her father be so <u>harsh</u>. She even offers to do some of the tasks herself. Of course, Ferdinand won't let her.

WOW! PEOPLE! AMAZING!

Wait till she sees what shops look like...

4) She's very <u>innocent</u>. The only people she's ever known until now are Prospero and Caliban (who's not exactly human anyway). She <u>falls in love</u> immediately with Ferdinand and offers to be his wife. When she meets Ferdinand's father Alonso and all his followers she's delighted to meet so many <u>new people</u>.

How beauteous mankind is! O brave new world That has such people in't!
Act 5, Scene 1, 183-184

Ferdinand and Miranda, sitting in a tree...

Aah, ain't they sweet? Miranda's been stuck on that island nearly her <u>whole life</u> without meeting any other young people — no wonder she falls for the <u>dishy</u> young Ferdinand. Although Prospero makes things hard for them, we know <u>true love</u> will win in the end. Someone pass me a bucket...

Caliban, Stephano and Trinculo

Unlike most of the other characters, these three are pretty <u>common</u>. They're quite <u>funny</u> too.

Caliban is Ugly and Deformed

1) Caliban was born on the island. His mother was Sycorax the <u>witch</u>.

2) He's <u>bitter</u> and <u>bad-tempered</u>. He says the island is his and Prospero has stolen it from him. He <u>curses</u> a lot, although in an entertaining kind of way.

I'm just having a bad hair day, that's all...

3) Prospero sees Caliban as a <u>savage animal</u> and treats him as a <u>slave</u>. Even sweet-hearted Miranda <u>can't stand him</u>.

4) Caliban is an ugly, earthly "<u>monster</u>", so he's very <u>different</u> from Ariel, who is light, airy and magical.

5) <u>Alcohol</u> has a funny effect on Caliban. When he becomes drunk, he calls Stephano a <u>god</u> and adopts him as his new <u>master</u>. He gets Stephano and Trinculo to join in his plan to <u>kill Prospero</u> and free him from his slavery.

Stephano is a Drunken Butler

1) Stephano has a stash of <u>wine</u> saved from the shipwreck. He's usually <u>drunk</u>, and he quickly gets Caliban and Trinculo drunk too.

2) He likes the attention he gets from Caliban and <u>takes charge</u> of the little group. The <u>power</u> seems to go to his head and at one point he gets <u>violent</u> with Trinculo.

3) He's <u>greedy</u> and tempted by the silly idea of being <u>king of the island</u>. He's <u>brash</u> and <u>confident</u> and doesn't realise how foolish he seems — until Ariel leads them into a <u>pond</u>, and their plot to kill Prospero <u>breaks down</u>.

Trinculo is a Jester

1) Like Stephano, Trinculo's <u>greedy</u> and <u>dishonourable</u>. He quickly joins in the plan to <u>kill Prospero</u>.

2) Trinculo's <u>witty</u> and <u>sarcastic</u> but also a bit of a <u>coward</u>. The way he describes Caliban is funny — he bickers and tries to <u>put him down</u>, but he's clearly a bit <u>frightened</u> of him too.

3) He's a fairly <u>weak</u> character. He fails to stand up for himself when Stephano <u>beats him up</u>, and generally does whatever Stephano says.

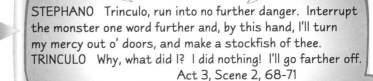

STEPHANO Trinculo, run into no further danger. Interrupt the monster one word further and, by this hand, I'll turn my mercy out o' doors, and make a stockfish of thee.
TRINCULO Why, what did I? I did nothing! I'll go farther off.
Act 3, Scene 2, 68-71

About as dangerous as a new-born kitten...

Stephano becomes the <u>leader</u> of this strange threesome — Caliban <u>worships</u> him and Trinculo's happy enough to <u>latch on</u> to them. They're all a bit sad really though — a bunch of <u>drunken</u> <u>weirdos</u> with an evil but badly thought out plan that predictably falls through. Good fun though.

16

The Less Important People

There are a few other characters who are there to help the story along.

The Ship's Crew Try to Fight the Storm

1) The Master is the captain of King Alonso's ship. He shouts instructions to the Boatswain.

2) The Boatswain is an officer on the ship. He works hard to save the ship during the storm. He gives orders to the crew of mariners and encourages them.

3) The Boatswain's loud and confident — when Sebastian and Antonio interfere during the storm, he shouts at them to go away and let him and his crew get on with it. He tries to save everyone during the storm, not just the King.

4) The Master, the Boatswain and the crew of mariners are the only ones who don't jump overboard during the storm. Ariel makes sure they're all right by putting a charm on them and taking the ship to a safe part of the island. At the end of the play they're ready to take everyone back to Italy.

Adrian and Francisco are Young Lords

Don't worry about us.

We're not very important.

1) They get washed ashore with the rest of Alonso's followers and they're just as confused.

2) They're fairly pleasant but don't really do much. Adrian chats to Gonzalo and ignores Sebastian and Antonio's rudeness. Francisco tries to give Alonso some hope — he tells him he saw Ferdinand swimming and he suggests he might have survived the storm.

3) When Sebastian, Antonio and Alonso all rush off looking for trouble, Gonzalo sends Adrian and Francisco after them to keep an eye on them.

The Island is Full of Spirits

1) The spirits can take on different forms and do what Prospero commands. Sometimes Prospero sends them to punish Caliban. They appear as apes, hedgehogs, hounds and adders. They frighten Caliban, hurt him and make him lose his way.

2) Prospero also uses his spirits to help make his enemies face up to their crimes. He makes them bring a banquet for Alonso and his group. The spirits appear in strange shapes and amaze the group.

3) The spirits perform in the masque (play) to celebrate the engagement of Ferdinand and Miranda. They take the forms of the goddesses Iris and Juno, with Ariel playing Ceres. Then some more spirits come and join in a dance.

Shakespearean pit workers — the miner characters...

It's unlikely you'll have to answer a question on any of these characters, but it's worth knowing how they fit into the story of the play. The spirits might seems a bit unrealistic, but just go with it.

Revision Summary

You need to be confident about who all the characters are and why they're important.
There are some pretty complicated relationships in there — once you've sussed out who
does what to who, you can get on with writing cracking essays. If you're not clear about
this stuff, studying the play will be harder than dragging Dawn French up Mount Snowdon
wearing flip-flops. Check you can answer all these questions.

1) Where did Prospero get his magic powers from?

    a) Studying books   b) A magical storm   c) Watching Paul Daniels on TV

2) How does Prospero show his tough side?

3) What does Prospero do to Antonio and Alonso at the end of the play?

4) Why does Ariel always do what Prospero tells him?

5) What powers does Ariel have?

6) What happens to Ariel in the end?

    a) Caliban kills him   b) Prospero sets him free   c) He becomes an accountant

7) What's Alonso's dodgy past?

8) How has Alonso changed by the end of the play?

9) How did Gonzalo help Prospero in the past?

10) Who does Gonzalo try to cheer up after the shipwreck?

11) Who's Antonio's brother?

12) Which of these is the best description of Antonio?

    a) A very nasty man   b) A loveable rogue   c) A top bloke

13) Who joins in with Antonio's plan to kill Alonso?

14) How does Ferdinand prove to Prospero that he's worthy of being Miranda's husband?

15) Why is Miranda so excited to meet new people?

16) Who was Caliban's mother?

17) Describe what Caliban looks like.

18) What's Stephano got a stash of?

    a) Weapons   b) Wine   c) Cheese   d) Golden Grahams

19) Who does Trinculo often argue with?

20) Who gets into a row with Sebastian and Antonio during the storm?

21) Who does Gonzalo tell to go off after Sebastian, Antonio and Alonso?

22) Describe three things the spirits do for Prospero.

23) What are the main differences between Ariel and Caliban?

Magic

Magic is <u>really important</u> in **The Tempest**. It's the <u>driving force</u> behind most of the main events of the play. Prospero uses it in <u>different ways</u> to make sure his <u>plans</u> run smoothly.

Prospero Controls the Magic

1) In Shakespeare's time lots of people believed in <u>witchcraft</u> and <u>magic</u>. This makes Prospero quite an <u>impressive</u> man — he claims he can dim the sun and even raise the dead. Even nasty Caliban <u>respects</u> and <u>fears</u> what Prospero can do.

2) Prospero's <u>good magic</u> is a contrast to the evil magic spells cast in the past by Caliban's mother <u>Sycorax</u>. One by one, Prospero's spells bring about a <u>happy ending</u>:

Drat, wrong spell again.

- He creates a <u>storm</u> (with Ariel's help). This brings Alonso and the others to the island, where Prospero has control over them.

- He sends Ariel to use <u>songs</u> and <u>charms</u> to bring Miranda and Ferdinand together. Ariel's music also wakes Gonzalo to <u>prevent Alonso being killed</u>.

- A <u>magical banquet</u> appears in front of Prospero's enemies, then vanishes, almost driving them mad.

- Prospero gets some spirits to perform a <u>masque</u> (play) for Ferdinand and Miranda. This is a <u>celebration</u> of their engagement and the <u>happiness</u> it will bring.

3) At the end of the play, Prospero holds his enemies in a <u>magic circle</u>. He has them completely in his power but he <u>forgives</u> them. He reveals who he is and reclaims his <u>rightful position</u> of Duke of Milan.

Even Prospero's Powers are Limited

1) Prospero's magic <u>doesn't</u> make him a god. He needed <u>good luck</u> and <u>Gonzalo's kindness</u> in order to survive his betrayal and wash up on the island.

2) He caused the storm and shipwreck — but he admits it was <u>good luck</u> that brought the ship near the island in the first place.

> By accident most strange, bountiful Fortune,
> Now my dear lady, hath mine enemies
> Brought to this shore
> Act 1, Scene 2, 179-181

3) He brings Ferdinand and Miranda together but their love is a <u>free choice</u>. He can't force it on them — they <u>choose</u> to get engaged. He can't force his enemies to <u>say sorry</u> either — Alonso does, but Antonio and Sebastian don't.

4) Prospero's powers come from the <u>magic clothes</u> and <u>books</u> Gonzalo gave him. When he gives these up at the end of the play, he is <u>giving up</u> his magic powers. But he chooses to do this because he <u>doesn't need</u> magic any more — he only used it to put things right.

Make English easy — now that would be magic...

Some of these magic events might seem rather unrealistic. But remember, The Tempest is a play so it needs to <u>look good</u> on the stage. Things like the shipwreck can really impress the audience. Honest.

Betrayal and Forgiveness

There's loads of <u>double-dealing</u> and <u>betrayal</u> in The Tempest. So what does Prospero do when he has the chance to take revenge on them all? He forgives them. Of course.

A Lot of Betrayal Happened Before the Play Starts

1) Prospero was betrayed by his <u>brother</u> Antonio when he was Duke of Milan. He trusted Antonio to help him govern. Antonio paid him back by <u>overthrowing</u> Prospero and <u>banishing</u> him and Miranda. Alonso and Sebastian were involved in the plot too.

2) Caliban says he was <u>betrayed by Prospero</u>. He claims that he showed Prospero around the island but then Prospero <u>took it over</u> as his own before making Caliban his <u>slave</u>.

There's Plenty of Plotting on the Island

1) Antonio and Sebastian plan to <u>kill</u> Sebastian's brother <u>Alonso</u>, so that Sebastian can take his position as <u>King of Naples</u>. It's initially Antonio's suggestion, but Sebastian happily goes along with it. This plot doesn't work though, and Alonso never finds out about it.

2) <u>Caliban</u> persuades Trinculo and Stephano to try and <u>kill</u> his master <u>Prospero</u>. He takes Stephano as his new master and tells him he could become <u>king of the island</u>.

3) Caliban's plot seems a lot <u>funnier</u> than Sebastian and Antonio's plot to kill Alonso, because of how <u>silly</u> Caliban, Stephano and Trinculo are.

Prospero Has a Lot to Forgive

1) We're <u>not sure</u> what Prospero will do with his enemies until the last minute. We don't know if he will <u>forgive</u> them or <u>punish</u> them. Ariel encourages him to be <u>merciful</u>, and Prospero agrees this is the honourable thing to do.

2) Prospero <u>forgives Alonso</u> for his part in the plot to betray him. Alonso feels really <u>sorry</u> for what he did, and Prospero accepts his apology.

> Though with their high wrongs I am struck to th'quick,
> Yet with my nobler reason 'gainst my fury
> Do I take part. The rarer action is
> In virtue than in vengeance.
> Act 5, Scene 1, 25-28

3) He even gives his approval for Miranda to marry Alonso's son, Ferdinand, and this is a sign that he's prepared to <u>forget the past</u>.

4) He <u>forgives Antonio</u> too — kind of. He's still angry, and says he <u>can't stand</u> to even call him his brother. Still, he does forgive him.

5) He's not even all that angry with <u>Caliban</u> for his evil plot — although Caliban will have to <u>work hard</u> to make up for it.

Someone's put me on a platter — I've been betrayed...

<u>Brotherly love</u> isn't very strong amongst this lot. My brother once broke my toy digger, but I got him back by selling his bike. Maybe I should have drawn a magic circle and forgiven him instead.

Justice and Fate

The story is about Prospero's plan to get justice — people getting what they deserve. This is linked to the idea of fate — some things are meant to be. It seems that justice is bound to be done.

Most of the Characters Get What They Deserve

1) Miranda and Ferdinand manage to pass Prospero's love test. Ferdinand does all the tasks he's set without complaining, and they don't sleep together before the wedding. So they are allowed to get married to each other — which is all they want.

2) Alonso thinks his son is dead for a lot of the play. His sadness might be seen as a punishment for what he did to Prospero. Once he has told Prospero how sorry he is, and given Prospero his dukedom back, Prospero repays him by revealing that Ferdinand is alive. Alonso's happiness is his reward for realising he did wrong.

> My dukedom since you have given me again,
> I will requite you with as good a thing,
> At least bring forth a wonder, to content ye
> As much as me my dukedom.
>
> Act 5, Scene 1, 168-171

3) Ariel has spent twelve years repaying Prospero for releasing him from Sycorax's spell. He has served him well — Prospero certainly keeps him busy. Ariel gets his freedom as soon as he has helped Prospero to achieve his plans.

Some Characters Don't Like What they Get

This was a respectable neighbourhood before you moved in...

Oh shut up and get tea ready.

1) Antonio and Sebastian are lucky that Prospero decides to forgive them. He doesn't even tell Alonso about their plot to kill him. They're not grateful though.

2) Trinculo and Stephano are left in a mucky pond for a while. Then they're chased off and pinched by spirits.

3) Caliban feels he's been treated unfairly. He claims that the island was originally his and Prospero stole it from him.

The Play Ends With Justice Being Done

1) Prospero says he was lucky that his enemies were brought close enough to his island for him to act. This suggests that fate was on his side.

2) It's perfect that Miranda and Ferdinand fall in love. Even Prospero couldn't guarantee that they would. It makes a firmer bond between Prospero and Alonso, and it brings Naples and Milan together. It seems that everyone will get on well in the future.

> When Prospero gets his rightful position of
> Duke of Milan back, justice is finally done.
> Things are as they once were, and as they should be.

"What's that on Prospero's head?"   "It's justice hat..."

The Tempest is a comedy, remember, so it needs a happy ending. And that means everyone getting what they deserve. In Shakespeare's time there was a strong belief in fate — there's no escaping what's meant to be, and Prospero was destined to be Duke of Milan again.

ACT 1 SCENES 1 & 2	**What Happens in Act One**

Straight to the action — the play starts off with a good old-fashioned <u>storm</u>.

Scene 1 — The shipwreck

1 A ship is caught in a tempest (storm)

A ship carrying Alonso (King of Naples), Sebastian (his brother), Ferdinand (Alonso's son), Antonio (Duke of Milan and Prospero's brother) and Gonzalo (an old man) is caught in a storm on the way back from the wedding of Alonso's daughter Claribel to the King of Tunis. The Boatswain encourages his crew to do their best to deal with the storm, and is annoyed when Alonso, Sebastian and Antonio come on to the deck to ask him questions. The Boatswain tells them to go back to their cabins. Antonio and Sebastian react angrily, but Gonzalo defends him. Lines 1-47

2 The crew prepare for the worst

The ship seems to be sinking, and Antonio says that the Boatswain is incompetent. Gonzalo hopes for the best. Lines 48-68

Scene 2 — Prospero talks about the past

Now we find out some important stuff about Prospero and Miranda's <u>past</u>.

1 Prospero says he's caused the storm

On the island, Miranda is worried about the ship she saw struggling in the storm. Her father, Prospero, says he raised the storm with his magic. He tells her not to worry, as he's made sure no one on the ship will come to any harm. Lines 1-33

2 Prospero tells Miranda about their past

Miranda has faint memories about her childhood, but can't remember much. Prospero tells her that twelve years ago, he used to be Duke of Milan. Then his brother, Antonio, abused Prospero's trust and raised an army with Alonso. They threw Prospero and Miranda (who was then very young) out of Milan, and Antonio took Prospero's title of Duke of Milan. Miranda is very upset by the story. Lines 33-136

3 Prospero continues his story

Prospero tells Miranda that the others put them both on an old boat and sent them out to sea. Fortunately, Gonzalo gave them food, clothes and some of Prospero's books, which he needs for his magic. By chance, they washed up on the island where they have been ever since. Miranda asks what this has got to do with the storm Prospero has raised, but Prospero says she is tired and should go to sleep. Lines 136-187 (Continued on next page)

"I used to be Duke of Milan, you know..."

Don't mistake Prospero's speech for the mad ravings of a bitter old man. What he says is <u>vital to the plot</u> — it's the whole reason he causes the storm that brings Alonso and his friends to the island. So make sure you know who's who and what they did in the past — it's dead important.

What Happens in Act One

Now we get to meet two rather weird characters, Prospero's <u>servants</u> Ariel and Caliban. Ariel's the good one, Caliban's all nasty and twisted (shudder).

Scene 2 (continued) — Prospero takes charge

4 Ariel reports to Prospero

Prospero calls for his servant, a spirit called Ariel. Ariel tells Prospero that he has done as he was told — he caused the storm, made the crew of Alonso's ship go mad trying to deal with it, but made sure no one was hurt. He scattered the survivors on different parts of the island, while the other ships in the fleet went back to Naples, thinking the King and his crew were dead. Lines 188-238

Can't I be free now?

It's SO unfair.

Not until you've done your homework.

5 Prospero gets angry with Ariel

Prospero says there is more work to do. When Ariel complains that Prospero promised to set him free, Prospero is annoyed and reminds him about the past. Ariel had been a servant of a horrible witch called Sycorax, who left Ariel imprisoned and then died. Ariel was in a terrible state, but Prospero rescued him, and made him his servant, along with Sycorax's deformed son Caliban. Prospero angrily tells Ariel to get on with the work he wants him to do, and Ariel goes off to do it. Lines 238-305

6 Caliban argues with Prospero

Miranda wakes up and goes with her father to see Caliban. Caliban bitterly argues with Prospero, who says he will punish him with painful spells. Caliban says he served Prospero well but was treated badly, but Prospero and Miranda say that Caliban behaved like a savage and deserves this treatment. Prospero orders Caliban to fetch fuel, and Caliban goes off to do it. Lines 306-376

Time for a bit of <u>romance</u> to cheer us up.

7 Ferdinand and Miranda fall in love

Ariel brings Ferdinand to Prospero and Miranda by singing to him. Ferdinand thinks his father, Alonso, and the other people who were on the ship, are dead. Ferdinand and Miranda instantly fall in love, and Prospero is pleased. Lines 377-452

At various points in the play, Ariel leads people to where Prospero wants them by singing and playing weird music to them.

8 Prospero decides to make things difficult

Prospero decides that their love has come too easily, so he decides to make things more difficult for them by accusing Ferdinand of being a traitor. He uses his magic to stop Ferdinand from fighting him, and says he will make him his slave. Miranda comforts Ferdinand. Prospero tells Ariel that after he has done more tasks he will be set free, before leading Ferdinand off to his work. Lines 453-504

That's no way to treat an England defender...

It might seem like Prospero's being a big old meanie to Ferdinand, but he really just wants to do what's right for his daughter. You can understand him being <u>suspicious</u> of young Ferdie — after all, his dad was involved in the whole usurping-Prospero-as-Duke-of-Milan business.

ACT 2 SCENE 1 — What Happens in Act Two

In this scene we see how the survivors deal with what's happened. It doesn't take Antonio and Sebastian long before they're plotting some nasty deeds...

Scene 1 — Sebastian and Antonio are up to no good

1 The survivors discuss what's happened

On a different part of the island, other people involved in the shipwreck talk about what has happened. Gonzalo tries unsuccessfully to cheer up Alonso by saying that at least they are still alive, while Sebastian and Antonio make fun of Gonzalo and Adrian (a lord who was on the ship). Gonzalo points out that, despite the storm, their clothes are as fresh as when they put them on. Lines 1-101

2 Alonso is very upset

Alonso wishes his daughter had never got married, as she now lives in Africa and his son Ferdinand is dead (or so he thinks). Francisco (another lord) tells Alonso he saw Ferdinand coping well with the storm and believes he is still alive, but Sebastian says Ferdinand must be dead. Gonzalo tells Sebastian he should be more tactful, before making a strange speech about what he would do if he was King of the island. Lines 102-182

My poor son must be dead.

Cheer up, he might have survived.

Nah he's dead — and it's all your fault.

As if there aren't enough plots to get your head around, Antonio and Sebastian now get in on the act.

Alonso's daughter Claribel is now in Africa, and everyone thinks his son Ferdinand is dead. So Sebastian, Alonso's brother, would become King of Naples if Alonso dies.

3 Antonio persuades Sebastian to kill Alonso

Ariel enters playing music, and eventually everyone but Sebastian and Antonio falls asleep, before Ariel leaves. Antonio then suggests to Sebastian that they should kill Alonso while he sleeps, so that Sebastian can take his place as King of Naples. At first, Sebastian is reluctant and worried about his conscience, but Antonio eventually convinces him. Lines 183-295

4 Ariel wakes Gonzalo just in time

Just as Sebastian and Antonio are about to kill Alonso, Ariel appears and wakes up Gonzalo, who wakes the others up. Sebastian and Antonio say they had their swords drawn because they thought there were lions about. Alonso says they should go and look for Ferdinand and leads them all away. Lines 296-326

Why don't you kill Alonso? Go on go on go on...

There's not much you can say in favour of Antonio and Sebastian, apart from that we really shouldn't be surprised. Alonso knows that Antonio is a traitor, because he helped him to betray Prospero years ago, so he can hardly expect Antonio to be trustworthy and loyal to him.

What Happens in Act Two

Stephano, Trinculo and Caliban get together and begin some drunken <u>shenanigans</u> — with hilarious consequences.

Scene 2 — Trinculo, Caliban and Stephano meet

1 Trinculo comes across Caliban

Caliban is out collecting wood, cursing the cruel things Prospero does to him. Then Trinculo (a jester from the ship) arrives, and Caliban tries to hide from him by covering himself with his cloak. Trinculo is looking for somewhere to take shelter from the storm that is approaching. He sees Caliban and takes shelter under his cloak — even though Caliban looks and smells awful. Lines 1-40

> What have we here? A man or a fish? Dead or alive? A fish — he smells like a fish — a very ancient and fish-like smell
>
> Act 2, Scene 2, 24-26

Things start getting a bit silly now...

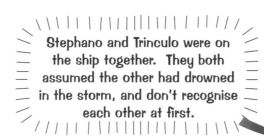

Stephano and Trinculo were on the ship together. They both assumed the other had drowned in the storm, and don't recognise each other at first.

2 Stephano thinks he's found a monster

Stephano (a butler from the ship) arrives, singing drunkenly. He comes across Caliban and thinks he is some kind of sick monster. Stephano gives Caliban some wine to try to make him better. Then Trinculo speaks up from under Caliban's cloak, and Stephano thinks the "monster" has two heads. Eventually Trinculo reveals himself and they tell each other how they escaped from the shipwreck. Then Stephano gives Trinculo some wine, telling him he's got a stash of it. Lines 41-132

3 Caliban thinks Stephano is a god

Because Stephano's drink has "healed" him, Caliban thinks Stephano is a god and offers to worship him and show him round the island. Stephano thinks this is funny and goes along with it. Caliban leads Stephano and Trinculo off, singing drunkenly. Lines 133-181

Hmm, these two look like a good laugh...

Show me the way to go home...

From this point on, Stephano, Trinculo and Caliban are always together, and they get into all sorts of <u>drunken mischief</u>. Stephano the butler seems glad to be in charge for once, with freaky Caliban looking up to him as a god and Trinculo the Not-Very-Funny Jester generally being a hanger-on.

ACT 3
SCENES 1 & 2

What Happens in Act Three

Love blossoms for Ferdinand and Miranda, while the troublemakers hatch an evil plan.

Scene 1 — Ferdinand and Miranda are in love

1 Miranda comforts Ferdinand while he works
Ferdinand is piling up logs as ordered by Prospero. Miranda comforts him and tells him her name. He says he loves her more than any other woman. Lines 1-48

2 Ferdinand and Miranda decide to get married
Miranda tells Ferdinand that she has met no other people apart from her father and Caliban, but she can't imagine that anyone would be better than Ferdinand. Prospero is watching them, and is pleased. Ferdinand and Miranda agree to get married. Lines 48-96

I love you, honeybunch.

Well colour me ginger and call me Cilla Black.

I love you too, shnookums.

Scene 2 — Trinculo, Caliban and Stephano are all drunk

1 Stephano turns on Trinculo
Stephano, Trinculo and Caliban are all drunk. Trinculo is nasty to Caliban, who asks Stephano, his "lord", to attack Trinculo. Caliban tells Stephano that Prospero stole his island. Ariel appears and says Caliban is lying, but Ariel is invisible, so Caliban and Stephano think Trinculo said it. When Ariel keeps saying Caliban is lying, Stephano beats Trinculo up. Lines 1-86

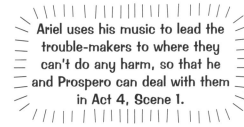
Ariel uses his music to lead the trouble-makers to where they can't do any harm, so that he and Prospero can deal with them in Act 4, Scene 1.

2 Caliban tells Stephano to kill Prospero
Caliban wants Stephano to kill Prospero, telling him he should first remove Prospero's books, so that he can't perform his magic. Caliban tells him that if Stephano kills Prospero, he can have Miranda, so Stephano agrees to do it. Lines 87-110

3 Ariel leads them away
Stephano apologises to Trinculo for beating him up, and the three of them sing, with Ariel providing the music. Caliban explains that the island is full of strange noises, and they walk off, following Ariel's music. Lines 111-152

I cut down trees, I press wild flowers...

Ah, young love... it seems that watching Ferdinand lug heavy objects around all day long just makes Miranda love him even more — funny that. Still at least she's not rushing into anything, waiting till their second date before agreeing to marry the first bloke she's ever met...

Section 4 — Understanding The Story

What Happens in Act Three

The shipwreck survivors continue to <u>suffer</u> on the island. The latest bush tucker trial involves a magically disappearing banquet, courtesy of Ariel.

Scene 3 — Alonso and his friends are having a hard time

1 Alonso gives up looking for Ferdinand
Gonzalo is tired from the search for Ferdinand, and Alonso says they should call it off. Antonio and Sebastian still intend to kill Alonso.
Lines 1-17

2 Ariel plays a trick
Some weird figures bring in a banquet. Alonso, Sebastian, Antonio and Gonzalo are amazed. Prospero watches them from above, unseen. Then Ariel appears in the form of a harpy and makes the banquet disappear. The men draw their swords but are unable to attack Ariel. Ariel reminds them of their past sins, and says they are getting what they deserve. Prospero is happy that everything is going as he has planned.
Lines 18-93

A harpy is a kind of monster with the wings and claws of a bird but the face of a woman. Ariel makes himself look like this to add to the other characters' fear and confusion.

3 Gonzalo tries to keep everyone calm
Alonso is sure Ferdinand is dead, and suspects Prospero is involved. He goes off in search of his son. Sebastian and Antonio also wander off to fight any enemies they can find. Gonzalo says they're all feeling guilty and tells the others to go and stop them doing anything foolish.
Lines 94-109

I fancy a ruck.

Me too.

Oh do be careful...

Never mind, you've always got your Formula 1 career...

He may not be the nicest man in the world, but I can't help feeling a bit sorry for poor old Alonso here. First his ship is washed up on a dead-end <u>island</u> in the middle of nowhere, then his son seems for all the world to have kicked the bucket, then a massive <u>feast</u> appears out of nowhere and disappears before he can have so much as a forkful. It's just going to be one of those days...

| ACT 4 SCENE 1 | # What Happens in Act Four |

Now Prospero starts tying up all the <u>loose ends</u> of his plans. First he gives Miranda and Ferdinand his blessing.

Scene 1 — The marriage can go ahead

1 Ferdinand and Miranda can get married
Prospero says Ferdinand has been tested enough, and gives his approval for him to marry Miranda. But he says that Ferdinand and Miranda had better not sleep together before they are married, or things will turn nasty. Ferdinand promises this won't happen. Lines 1-32

> All thy vexations
> Were but my trials of thy love, and thou
> Hast strangely stood the test.
> Act 4, Scene 1, 5-7

2 A play is performed
Prospero tells Ariel to summon some other spirits to perform a masque (a kind of play). The goddesses Iris, Ceres and Juno, played by spirits, appear and talk about health, love and prosperity. Lines 33-138

Just when everyone's relaxing, Prospero remembers something.

3 Prospero and Ariel deal with Caliban
Prospero suddenly remembers Caliban's plot to kill him, and cuts the masque short. Ferdinand and Miranda are surprised, but Prospero tells them not to worry about him. Ariel takes Prospero to where he left Stephano, Trinculo and Caliban, in a filthy lake nearby. Ariel hangs some fancy clothes on a nearby tree to trick them. Lines 139-193

4 The troublemakers are chased off
Unseen, Prospero and Ariel watch Caliban, Stephano and Trinculo, who are muddy and annoyed. Trinculo and Stephano try on some of the clothes hanging on the tree. Caliban tells them they should get on with killing Prospero, but they tell him to carry some clothes away. Then they hear the sounds of a hunt, and Prospero and Ariel, leading the hunt, appear and chase them off. Lines 194-265

I thought this was banned now?

TALLY-HO!

Time to take out the trash...

Don't you just hate it when you're settling down to watch some spirits perform a weird play, then you realise you've forgotten to foil a <u>plot against your life</u> led by a bunch of weirdos? Happens to me all the time. Never mind, looks like good old Prospero's got everything in hand.

What Happens in Act Five

Just to show what a great guy he is, Prospero gets everyone together, casts a <u>spell</u> on them, and tells them they're aaaaall right.

Scene 1 — Prospero forgives his enemies

1 Ariel reports to Prospero

Ariel tells Prospero that Alonso and his followers are all being held in a nearby lime grove. Ariel says they are all out of their minds with worry and asks Prospero to be kind to them. Prospero says he intends to forgive them all. Lines 1-32

2 Prospero casts a spell

Prospero draws a magic circle on the floor, saying this will be the last time he ever uses magic. Ariel brings the King and his followers to Prospero, and they are held under a spell in the circle. Prospero, invisible to the others, praises Gonzalo but criticises Alonso and his brother Sebastian for their part in his downfall, before forgiving them. Prospero removes his magician's clothes and instructs Ariel to fetch the master and the Boatswain from the ship. Lines 33-103

3 Prospero reveals himself and forgives all

Prospero reveals who he is to the other characters and welcomes Alonso with a hug. Alonso and Gonzalo can't quite believe it's Prospero. Prospero then says he forgives Antonio and Sebastian, even though he is still angry about what they did. Lines 104-134

4 Prospero reveals Ferdinand and Miranda

Alonso asks Prospero how he is still alive, then mentions how upset he is about the loss of his son Ferdinand. Prospero says that he lost his daughter in the storm. He then reveals Miranda and Ferdinand, playing chess. Alonso is delighted, and Miranda is thrilled to see so many new people. Ferdinand tells Alonso that Miranda is the daughter of the Duke of Milan, and Alonso happily accepts her as his daughter-in-law. Gonzalo and Prospero thank the gods for the way things have turned out. Lines 134-215 (continued on next page)

> O wonder!
> How many goodly creatures are there here!
> How beauteous mankind is! O brave new world
> That has such people in't!
>
> Act 5, Scene 1, 181-184

And that's magic...

Hmm, I think if I was a magician I'd do something a bit more fun, like turning people into ostriches or moving Huddersfield to Egypt. But Prospero's an honest, responsible chap, and with his last spell he reveals that no harm's been done and he <u>forgives everyone</u>. What a nice man.

| ACT 5 SCENE 1 & EPILOGUE |
What Happens in Act Five

I can feel a <u>happy ending</u> coming on...

Scene 1 (continued) — They prepare to return to Milan

5 The Boatswain says the ship is fine

Ariel brings the master and the Boatswain from the ship. The Boatswain says the ship is in good condition. Alonso says it's all very strange and asks the Boatswain how he got there. The Boatswain says he doesn't know — it was like a horrible dream, then they woke up and the boat looked fine, and they were brought to where they are now. Prospero thanks Ariel and says he will set him free. Alonso asks again what has happened, but Prospero says he'll tell him all about it later. Lines 216-253

It's all back to Prospero's before the big <u>journey home</u>.

YES! Free at last.

DOH! I'm still a freak.

THE END

I'm going home — ROCK 'N' ROLL!

6 Prospero releases the troublemakers

Prospero tells Ariel to release Stephano, Trinculo and Caliban from the spell they've been under. Ariel brings them over. Sebastian and Antonio don't recognise them at first, and find their terrible, drunken condition very funny. Prospero reveals Caliban's plot against him, then Alonso and Sebastian recognise Stephano and Trinculo. Prospero orders Caliban, Stephano and Trinculo away. Caliban curses himself for worshipping Stephano. Lines 253-304

7 Prospero invites everyone back to his cave

Prospero invites Alonso and his followers back to his cave, where he says he will tell them the whole story of what happened to him. The next day they will sail to Naples for Ferdinand and Miranda's wedding, then Prospero will go back to Milan. Lines 305-323

Epilogue — Prospero talks to the audience

Prospero prepares to go home

Prospero says he has now given up his magic. He asks for support on his journey home. Lines 1-20

Prospero is alone on the stage for the epilogue. He speaks directly to the audience, rather than any other characters.

And they all lived happily ever after...

So there you are, it all worked out in the end. Told you it would. Some people reckon Prospero's epilogue was Shakespeare's <u>farewell speech</u> to the theatre. Me, I don't know — I just hope he doesn't get back to Milan just to find he's left the bathroom light on all these years.

Revision Summary

I bet you've been looking forward to this page. Yep that's right, lots of lovely questions to test how much you understand the play. This might not be much fun, but if you don't know what happens you won't get anywhere when you have to take an exam on it. So give it your best shot — you'll feel a lot better when you've worked out what bits you understand and what bits you don't.

1) Describe three magical events that happen in the play.

2) Can Prospero use magic to do anything he wants?

3) Who betrayed who before the play starts?

4) Describe two nasty plots that are going on during the play.

5) How is justice done for Alonso?

6) Why does Caliban feel he's been treated unfairly?

7) Name five people who were on the ship in Act 1, Scene 1.

8) What title did Prospero have in the past?

   a) King of Naples   b) Duke of Milan   c) Earl of Slough

9) Why does Prospero lose his temper with Ariel in Act 1, Scene 2?

10) How does Prospero make things difficult for Ferdinand and Miranda?

11) Who tries to cheer Alonso up after the shipwreck?

12) Who do Antonio and Sebastian plan to kill?

   a) Alonso   b) Prospero   c) Gonzalo

13) Why does Trinculo crawl under Caliban's cloak?

14) Why does Caliban think Stephano is a god?

15) Who's watching Ferdinand and Miranda when they decide to get married? How does he react?

16) What does Caliban want Stephano to do in Act 3, Scene 2?

17) Describe the trick Ariel plays in Act 3, Scene 3.

18) What's Prospero's happy news in Act 4, Scene 1?

19) Why does Prospero cut the masque short?

   a) He has to take care of Caliban's plot against him.

   b) To save Alonso from Sebastian and Antonio.

   c) Because Big Brother is about to start.

20) What does Prospero say to Antonio and Sebastian after releasing them from the spell in Act 5, Scene 1?

21) What game are Ferdinand and Miranda playing when Prospero reveals them to Alonso?

   a) Hopscotch   b) Chess   c) British Bulldogs

22) What state is the ship in, according to the Boatswain?

23) What promise does Prospero make to Ariel in Act 5, Scene 1?

24) Where will Miranda and Ferdinand's wedding take place?

25) What does Prospero plan to do after the wedding?

Three Steps for an Essay

So you've had a good look at the play. In this section we'll look at the kind of essay you'll have to write, and some good tips for getting really good marks in the test.

Three Steps to Exam Success

These three steps are perfect for answering exam questions.
And they work for any kind of Shakespeare question — bargain.

1) Read the question and underline the important bits.

2) Go through the set scenes and look for examples you could use in your answer.

3) Do a quick plan for your essay. Look back at this when you're writing so you don't run out of ideas.

See pages 33-34 for more about planning.

The Question Will Look Like This

Whichever question type you get, the basic layout will look like this:

The Tempest

Act 2 Scene 1, lines 98-131
Act 3 Scene 3, lines 1-102

This bit tells you which parts of the play the question is about. It'll be about half the set scenes (printed on pages 49-56 of this book).

There might be a bit like this to introduce the topic of the question.

In these scenes, Alonso faces some disturbing situations.

What do Alonso's reactions to his problems reveal about his character?

Support your ideas by referring to both of the extracts which are printed on the following pages.

18 marks

This basically means "keep looking at the scenes and include loads of quotes".

This is the really important bit — the actual question. It's important that you read this carefully, so that you fully understand what you're being asked.

Steps? I thought they'd split up...

Although there are a few different types of question (see Section 6), they all pretty much follow the same format as the one on this page. So get familiar with it and you'll know what to expect.

Using Quotes

For every point you make, you have to back it up by using a <u>quote</u>. Quotes prove your points — if you don't use them, you've got no <u>proof</u> that you're not just making it up.

Keep the Quotes Short

Keep quotes <u>short</u> and <u>to the point</u> — a couple of lines is usually enough.

e.g. *Straight after the shipwreck, Alonso seems to be a rather pessimistic character. When Gonzalo tries to cheer him up, Alonso refuses to take any comfort from his words:*
"You cram these words into mine ears against
The stomach of my sense."   Act 2, Scene 1, 104-105

Start a new <u>paragraph</u>.

Copy down the <u>exact</u> words.

Say <u>where</u> the quote comes from. Give the <u>act</u>, <u>scene</u>, and <u>line numbers</u>.

If the quote's less than a line you <u>don't</u> need to put it in a separate paragraph or say where the quote's from, but you <u>do</u> need to put it in speech marks.

e.g. *Alonso believes there is no chance Ferdinand survived the storm, believing he must have drowned. He says "My son is lost".*

Explain Why the Quote is Relevant

1) Remember to make it really clear <u>why</u> you've included the quotes — don't just stick them in and expect the examiner to see the point you're making.

e.g. *When Alonso first sees the banquet, he is taken in completely. He excitedly says "Give us kind keepers, Heavens!", and sounds delighted. After the food vanishes, however, he says it is a "monstrous" situation. This suggests he is quite emotional, changing from one strong feeling to another in a short space of time.*

These quotes are good because they show something about <u>Alonso's character</u>, which is what the question's about.

I'll have an onion bhaji to start...

2) Quote <u>different characters</u> — this makes your answer more <u>interesting</u>. E.g. You could include Sebastian's view that Alonso has brought a lot of his troubles on himself.

3) Remember though that characters will have particular <u>reasons</u> for saying certain things — don't assume they're being totally honest and fair.

Status Quote — the studious rock band...

So the main points about quoting are: 1) Keep 'em <u>short</u>. 2) <u>Explain</u> how they answer the question. This'll make sure the quotes really <u>add</u> something to your answer.

Planning and Structure

If you <u>plan</u> your essay first, you'll have <u>more</u> chance of getting loads of <u>marks</u>.

You Need a Beginning, a Middle and an End

A good essay has a <u>beginning</u>, a <u>middle</u> and an <u>end</u>.
Just like a good story.

Just like me then.

1) The <u>hardest</u> part is <u>beginning</u> your essay. The <u>first sentence</u> has to start <u>answering</u> the question, and tell the examiner that your essay is going to be good. All that from <u>one</u> sentence — so you'd better start <u>practising</u>.

2) The middle part of your essay <u>develops</u> your <u>argument</u> — this is where you make all your points. Follow your plan.

3) The end <u>sums up</u> the points you've made and <u>rounds</u> the essay <u>off</u> nicely.

Before You Write, Make a Plan

I wish I was organised...

Planning means <u>organising</u> your material to help you write a clear answer that makes sense. A good plan turns that <u>heap of ideas</u> in your head into an <u>argument</u> supported by <u>points</u>.

Planning might seem a <u>pain</u> to do, but if you do it, you'll be <u>less</u> likely to get <u>lost</u> halfway through the essay.

Five Steps to Planning a Good Essay

1) Work out <u>exactly</u> what the question is asking you to do. Find the <u>key words</u> and underline them.

2) Read the <u>set scenes</u> — highlight <u>quotations</u> you could use.

3) Jot down your <u>ideas</u> — from the set scenes they <u>give</u> you, and from your <u>knowledge</u> of the <u>rest</u> of the play — and then put them into an <u>order</u>.

4) Decide what your <u>opinion</u> is, and how you can <u>use</u> your points to <u>support</u> it — to form an <u>argument</u>. Put your <u>best</u> point <u>first</u>.

5) Don't stick to your plan <u>rigidly</u>. If you think of any more <u>good ideas</u> once you've started writing, then try to fit them in.

It's the beginning of the end...

If you're not sure what your <u>opinion</u> is, state the arguments <u>for and against</u>, and give evidence to support each viewpoint. Answer the question by <u>comparing</u> the views on <u>each side</u>.

Planning and Structure

Here's an example of how you could make a plan for a question on The Tempest.

Work Out What the Question is Asking

e.g. Act 1 Scene 2, lines 321-373 and Act 3 Scene 2, lines 20-103
In these scenes we learn about Caliban's character.
What impressions of Caliban do we get from these scenes?
Support your ideas by referring to the scenes.

1) Start by <u>underlining</u> the most <u>important</u> words in the question.
For this one you'd underline "impressions" and "Caliban".

2) Once you've got the question in your head, go through the scenes and <u>pick out sections</u> of the scenes that look like they'll help your answer.

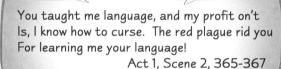

You taught me language, and my profit on't
Is, I know how to curse. The red plague rid you
For learning me your language!
Act 1, Scene 2, 365-367

3) Go through the scenes again and check for things you <u>might have missed</u> — it looks really good if you can find points that are <u>relevant</u> but <u>not obvious</u>.

Making Your Plan

Next jot down a <u>plan</u> for your essay. <u>Don't</u> bother writing in proper English in your plan — just get your ideas down.

This essay is all about <u>Caliban</u>, so make notes on <u>anything</u> from the scenes you think tells us something about Caliban.

Decide on the best <u>order</u> for your points.

Write down any <u>comments</u> you've got on what happens.

Find some <u>good quotes</u> to back up your points.

Impressions of Caliban

1. *He's ugly and deformed* Prospero calls Caliban "Hag-seed" and Stephano thinks he's a "monster".

3. 2. *He's weird and comical* Even though he often tries to do bad things, Caliban actually comes across as quite funny — Stephano calls him "Mooncalf".

2. 3. *He's immoral* Caliban's bitter that Prospero "cheated me of this island", and wants Stephano to kill Prospero. Also, Prospero accuses him of trying to rape Miranda.

My essay blossomed — I plant it well...

<u>Don't</u> just launch straight in — take the <u>time</u> to plan. Once you've <u>jotted</u> some ideas down, you'll realise you have <u>more</u> to say than you thought — so there's <u>less</u> reason to <u>panic</u>. And let's face it, a <u>structured</u> essay will get more marks than one that goes <u>all over the place</u>...

Writing Your Answer

Once you've got a plan, you're <u>ready</u> to start writing.
Make your points as <u>clearly</u> as you can so the examiner knows what you're on about.

Write a Simple Opening Paragraph

Start by using the exact <u>words of the task</u> in your introduction.
This shows you've <u>understood</u> the question.

Your introduction <u>doesn't</u> have to be <u>long</u> at all. It's just there to show what your <u>basic</u> <u>answer</u> to the task is. In the rest of the paragraphs you'll need to go into <u>detail</u>.

> <u>What impressions of Caliban do we get from these scenes?</u>
>
> In <u>these scenes</u> we get a strong <u>impression</u> of <u>Caliban</u>'s personality and appearance. He seems to be an ugly, deformed creature, capable of appalling behaviour, yet he also seems a comical character.
>
> We are first introduced to Caliban when Prospero describes him as...

The opening sentences use words from the <u>question</u>.

Once you've written your opening paragraph, just follow the order of your <u>plan</u> to write the rest of your essay.

Make Your Answer Interesting

1) Use <u>interesting</u> words — the examiner will get <u>bored</u> if you <u>overuse</u> dull words and phrases like "nice" and "I think". Try using words like "<u>fascinating</u>" and phrases like "<u>in my opinion</u>".

2) Keep your style <u>formal</u> — this makes your argument more <u>convincing</u> and gets you even more <u>marks</u>.

3) If you think a passage is "poetic", "realistic" etc., remember to explain <u>exactly why</u> — with examples. <u>Don't</u> assume it's <u>obvious</u> to the examiner.

Boring!

It was a nice day, and everyone had a nice time.

Keep bearing in mind the <u>words</u> used in the <u>question</u>. Using them in your essay will show you're <u>keeping to the task</u> and not getting lost.

Allow me to introduce my lovely essay...

Your intro really doesn't need to be anything mindblowing. Just a couple of sentences to show you've <u>understood</u> the question and to get your answer started. Then you start moving onto more <u>detailed</u> points in the rest of your answer, with some nice tasty <u>quotes</u> to back them up.

Concluding and Checking for Errors

Once you've made <u>all</u> your points, you need to <u>sum up</u> your answer and <u>check</u> it through.

Write a <u>Conclusion</u> to Sum Up Your <u>Key Points</u>

The conclusion to my speech will be very concise — barely half an hour...

1) Start a new <u>paragraph</u> for your conclusion.

2) Sum up the <u>main points</u> of your essay <u>briefly</u>. This makes it clear how you've <u>answered</u> the question.

3) Don't go on and on, though. It's best if your conclusion is just a <u>couple of sentences</u>.

Go Over <u>Your Essay</u> When You've Finished

1) Try to <u>leave time</u> at the end to <u>read through</u> your essay quickly. Check that it <u>makes sense</u>, that you haven't got any facts wrong, and that it says what you <u>want</u> it to say.

2) Check the <u>grammar</u>, <u>spelling</u> and <u>punctuation</u>. If you find a <u>mistake</u>, put <u>brackets</u> round it, cross it out <u>neatly</u> with two lines through it and write the <u>correction</u> above.

How many more times do I have to go over it?

> bitter
> Caliban is very (~~biter~~) towards Prospero

Don't <u>scribble</u> or put <u>whitener</u> on mistakes — it looks <u>messy</u> and you'll <u>lose marks</u>.

3) If you've written something which isn't <u>clear</u>, put an <u>asterisk</u> * at the end of the sentence. Put another asterisk in the <u>margin</u>, and write what you <u>mean</u> in the margin.

> *He uses him as a slave. | Prospero seems to treat Caliban badly*.

Don't Panic <u>if You Realise You've Gone Wrong</u>

If you realise you've <u>forgotten</u> something really <u>obvious</u> and <u>easy</u>, then write a <u>note</u> about it at the bottom of the <u>final</u> page, to tell the examiner. If there's time, write an extra <u>paragraph</u>. You'll pick up marks for <u>noticing</u> your mistake.

> <u>Don't give up</u> if you're running out of <u>time</u> — even if you only have <u>five minutes</u> left, that's still time to pick up <u>extra marks</u>.

Check, check, check — I must be rich...

You've almost <u>finished</u>. Keep your conclusions <u>to the point</u>, and <u>check</u> your essay so you don't <u>throw away</u> marks on <u>silly mistakes</u>. Keep a <u>clear head</u> right up to the end — then it's <u>teatime</u>.

Revision Summary

I like to think of it as the 5 Ps — Planning Prevents Pitifully Poor Performance. Actually, I think it's a bit more positive than that — Planning Provides Practically Perfect Performance. The main point is Planning Planning Planning Planning Planning. Anyway, that's enough Ps for now. On with the revision summary — you only know the answers when you don't have to flick back.

1) Name three useful things you should do before you start writing an answer to an exam question.

2) Why is it important to use lots of quotes in your essay?

3) What three bits of information do you have to give after any quote that's more than a line long?

4) What punctuation marks do you use on quotes that are shorter than one line?

5) What should you explain about every quote you use?

6) What are the three vital ingredients of a good essay?
a) Spelling, handwriting and punctuation.
b) Great ideas, brilliant ideas and fantastic ideas.
c) A beginning, a middle and an end.

7) What's the big advantage of making a plan for an essay question?

8) If you have a great idea when you're writing your essay which wasn't on your original plan, is it OK to fit it into your essay anyway?

9) How important is it to write your plan in proper English?

10) What do you have to do with the first sentence of the answer?
a) Give a general answer to the question.
b) Make your best point straightaway.
c) Put in a really interesting quote.

11) Should you use mostly formal language or mostly slang in your answer?

12) How long should your closing paragraph be?
a) About half a page.
b) As long as a piece of string.
c) As short as possible but it should include all the main points from the essay.

13) Write down four things you should check for when you read through your essay at the end.

14) How do you correct a spelling mistake?

15) What should you do if you've written something which isn't clear?

How do you spell "clueless"?

| CHARACTER QUESTIONS | ## Questions About a Character |

You might be asked a question about a particular <u>character</u> in The Tempest.

Character Questions are Fairly Simple

Questions about a character will often ask you <u>what the scenes show</u> about that person.

> **Act 1 Scene 2, lines 242-330 and Act 5 Scene 1, lines 95-134**
> In these scenes we learn about Prospero's character.
> **How do these scenes show different sides of Prospero's character?**
> *Support your ideas by referring to the scenes.*

When you first read through the question, remember to <u>underline</u> the words which seem the <u>most important</u>.

<u>How</u> do these scenes show <u>different sides</u> of <u>Prospero's character</u>?

You have to explain how Shakespeare shows there are different sides to Prospero.

These words are the most important ones. They tell you what to write about.

They're Not all Goodies and Baddies

1) The characters in The Tempest are often more <u>complicated</u> than they seem.

2) Take Prospero. It's fair to say that overall he's a <u>good bloke</u>. He <u>loves</u> his daughter, he <u>forgives</u> people who've done the dirty on him, and what's more he can decide what the <u>weather</u>'s going to be like — pretty impressive.

And the outlook for today, a massive storm that will bring all my old enemies to the island...

3) BUT — he keeps Caliban as a <u>slave</u>, puts Ferdinand through <u>hell</u>, and he's even quite <u>harsh</u> on Ariel for a while too.

4) He says he's got <u>good reason</u> for all of these things, and he may have a point. But if you write about Prospero, <u>don't</u> make out he's perfect. Question <u>why</u> he does things, and remember that <u>not everyone</u>'s all that keen on him.

5) And then there's <u>Ferdinand</u>. He's the <u>son</u> of mean old <u>Alonso</u>, so you might expect him to be a bit of a cad too. But Ferdinand turns out to be a <u>straight-up</u>, <u>hard-working</u> fella. It just goes to show...

That Prospero, eh? What a character...

These questions shouldn't ask you anything <u>unexpected</u> — you should know about the characters and their odd little ways before the exam. Try to be really <u>thorough</u> and there'll be no hiccups.

Characters — The Bigger Picture

If you're asked to write about a <u>character</u> there are <u>a few things</u> you can do to get <u>more marks</u> — it's a question of looking for the <u>less obvious</u> things.

Think About What Motivates the Characters

1) <u>Motivation</u> means the <u>reasons</u> a character has for acting as they do.

2) The characters in The Tempest are all after <u>different things</u>. Some people are driven by <u>good intentions</u>, some by <u>bad intentions</u>. Some of them do things for <u>themselves</u>, some do things for <u>others</u>.

3) Try to show in your answer that you understand what <u>motivates</u> the character you're writing about. Again, find a good <u>quote</u> and say what it tells you about the character:

e.g.

Prospero calls himself "The wronged Duke of Milan", which shows he thinks he has been treated unfairly. Prospero is saying that the reason he brought the "traitors" to the island is that he wants justice to be done, rather than because he just wants more power for himself.

Remember What Happened in the Past

1) We know <u>more</u> about the characters than just the stuff that happens <u>during</u> the play. Things that happened in the <u>past</u> affect how the characters act towards each other in the play.

2) There's a lot of <u>history</u> between <u>Prospero</u>, his brother <u>Antonio</u>, and <u>Alonso</u>. We <u>don't see</u> Alonso behaving all that badly, but we know that he <u>betrayed</u> <u>Prospero</u> in the past.

3) The history between Prospero and his <u>servants</u> is important too. Caliban claims that Prospero <u>stole</u> the island from him when he first arrived. Prospero disagrees — he says he treated him well until Caliban <u>tried it on</u> with Miranda.

This island's mine, by Sycorax my mother, Which thou tak'st from me.
Act 1, Scene 2, 333-334

4) Prospero also uses the past to justify his demands of <u>Ariel</u>. He <u>rescued</u> Ariel from the witch Sycorax — and he won't let him forget it...

Have a good look at pages 9-16 for more details on the characters. Read pages 21-29 for a summary of what happens in the whole play.

Bill Shakes-beer — the nervous pub landlord...

So that's one type of exam question. Writing about characters is probably the <u>simplest</u> of the four kinds of question we'll look at. On the next two pages we'll look at writing about language.

How Language Is Used

If you're asked about Shakespeare's "use of language", it just means <u>what words he uses</u>.

Language Can Tell us About Characters

The kind of words each character uses affects our <u>impression</u> of them.

1) Miranda's language shows us how <u>amazed</u> she is just at seeing <u>new people</u>. This emphasises how <u>young</u> and <u>innocent</u> she is.

2) The <u>formal language</u> of Prospero's spells make him appear <u>wise</u> and <u>powerful</u> — he describes his magic as "my so potent art".

> O wonder!
> How many goodly creatures are there here!
> How beauteous mankind is!
> Act 5, Scene 1, 181-183

3) Caliban, on the other hand, is <u>foul-mouthed</u> and <u>bitter</u> — even he says that the only thing he gained from learning to speak was knowing "how to curse". This adds to the idea that he is an <u>uncivilised monster</u>.

Language is Used to Tell the Story

I used to be important you know!

Yeah yeah, whatever.

1) The language used to describe the <u>past</u> affects our view of what happened.

2) We find out about the past when <u>Prospero</u> tells Miranda about how he was "betrayed".

3) Prospero's <u>choice of words</u>, e.g. describing Antonio as "perfidious" (scheming), means we see things from <u>Prospero's point of view</u>.

4) This means we get a <u>biased</u> view of the past, rather than a neutral description.

Language can be Used to Create Comedy

Most of the funny bits in The Tempest involve Stephano, Trinculo and Caliban. The language they use creates a <u>comical</u>, <u>light-hearted</u> atmosphere.

e.g. Lo, lo again! Bite him to death, I prithee.
Act 3, Scene 2, 33

All three of them are <u>drunk</u> by this point, and Caliban's <u>animal-like</u> language makes him seem even more <u>silly</u>. It adds to the comedy of the scene.

As long as it's not in Swedish, you'll be fine...

Studying Shakespeare is really <u>all about</u> looking at what language he uses. So if you get a question that asks you specifically about his <u>choice of words</u>, there should be <u>plenty</u> you can write about.

How Language Creates Mood

"Mood" or "atmosphere" means the <u>feel</u> of a scene — whether it's tense, funny, exciting or whatever. You might be asked about <u>how language is used</u> to create a particular <u>mood</u>.

Say What Effect the Words Create

 Act 1 Scene 1, whole scene and Act 5 Scene 1, lines 104-171
How does Shakespeare's choice of language create a tense mood in these scenes?

Make it tense...
How about some snakes? No...

Use words from the question.

In the first scene, <u>Shakespeare's choice of language creates a tense mood</u> by giving the impression of people shouting in a panic-stricken way. For example, phrases like "All lost!" <u>bring home the drama of the storm and the fear</u> felt by the people who are caught up in it. When the Boatswain shouts "Lay her a-hold!", <u>it creates a sense of the crew desperately trying to save the ship</u>, unsure of whether they will survive or not.

In Act 5 Scene 1, the tension is created by angrier, more accusing language. Prospero refers to Sebastian and Antonio as "<u>traitors</u>" and addresses his brother Antonio as "<u>most wicked sir</u>". This shows his anger at being betrayed, <u>adding to the tension between the characters</u>.

Say how the language creates a certain effect.

Explain the exact effect of the language.

Quote loads.

Keep the answer focused and to-the-point.

Look for Mood Changes Within Scenes

It'll add a little <u>extra</u> to your answer if you can identify the place where the mood of a scene <u>changes</u>. For example, if you were writing about Act 4, Scene 1, you could say something like:

The language in the first part of the scene creates a happy atmosphere. The goddesses in the masque talk about "<u>Honour, riches, marriage-blessing</u>", adding to the sense of celebration at Ferdinand and Miranda's engagement.

However, <u>the mood changes completely when Prospero remembers the plot against him</u>. This is shown by the language used, as talk of happiness and fertility turns to the problem of Caliban's "<u>foul conspiracy</u>".

Show how the language reflects the change.

Say where the change in mood happens.

Heaven knows I'm miserable now... but not now...

So there's quite a bit you can write about for these questions to please the examiner. They give you the opportunity to really go to town and show off your <u>understanding</u> of the language.

Writing About a Theme

Theme questions sound more tricky than they really are. They're generally just asking <u>how</u> the play puts across a particular <u>message</u> or <u>idea</u>.

Work Out What the Question is Asking

<u>Theme questions</u> are often worded like this:

> **Act 1 Scene 2, lines 66-132 and Act 3 Scene 3, lines 53-82**
>
> In these scenes, Prospero and Ariel describe how Alonso and his followers betrayed Prospero's trust in order to gain power.
>
> **How do these extracts explore the idea that people must pay for their crimes?**
>
> *Support your ideas by referring to the scenes.*

<u>Don't panic</u> if the question seems complicated.

Read it carefully, and you'll realise it's actually pretty <u>simple</u>.

> You could rephrase this as:
> "These bits of the play show that people will pay for their crimes. How do they do this?"

Theme Questions Aren't as Hard as They Look

1) Read through the scenes with the question in mind, and some points should pretty much <u>leap out</u> at you and give you the <u>basis for a good answer</u>. For example, for the question above, this quote from <u>Ariel</u> would be useful:

> you three
> From Milan did supplant good Prospero,
> Exposed unto the sea, which hath requit it,
> Him, and his innocent child, for which foul deed
> The pow'rs, delaying, not forgetting, have
> Incensed the seas and shores, yea, all the creatures,
> Against your peace.
>
> Act 3, Scene 3, 69-75

You're nicked.

2) Once you've found a good extract like this, just say <u>how it relates to the question</u>. Don't forget to stick in some good <u>quotes</u> to back up your points:

> Ariel reminds Alonso and his followers that they "did supplant good Prospero" in the past. He then makes it clear that their current predicament is a direct punishment for this "foul deed".

I don't like extracts — they remind me of dentists...

Questions about themes generally <u>tell you</u> an opinion, then ask you to <u>prove</u> that it's true. Which makes it <u>easy</u> really — no faffing about deciding what to argue, just find some good <u>evidence</u>.

Themes You Might be Asked About

Here are a few more things you can do if you get a question about a <u>theme</u> or <u>issue</u> in The Tempest.

There are Several Themes in The Tempest

If you do get a <u>theme question</u>, it's likely to be about one of the following:

- fate and justice
- magic
- love
- freedom
- betrayal and forgiveness
- slavery and service

It's worth having a think about these themes and working out <u>what you'd write</u> about them. Have a look at pages 18-20 for more about the <u>themes</u> in The Tempest.

Look for the Less Obvious Bits

1) There will usually be plenty of fairly <u>obvious points</u> you can use in your answer to a theme question (like the stuff on the previous page).

2) But if you want to get really <u>great marks</u>, you'll need to go into a bit more <u>detail</u>. Try to write something that answers the question in a way that's <u>not</u> immediately obvious.

> *Maybe Prospero himself was only getting what he deserved when he lost his position as Duke of Milan. He admits that he was so obsessed with learning that he became guilty of "neglecting worldly ends". This seems to be what allowed Antonio's "falsehood" to develop — if Prospero had paid more attention to his duties, it is possible that Antonio would not have had the chance to abuse his trust.*

3) It's especially important that you give <u>evidence</u> for these kinds of points. The examiner might not have thought of this, so it's <u>vital</u> you back it up with good <u>quotations</u>.

4) Don't go <u>over the top</u> trying to write blindingly original stuff — make sure you don't miss out the <u>clear-cut</u> points that'll give you easy marks. But if you can stick in just <u>one or two</u> more unexpected, well-explained points into your plan, along with the easier stuff, they'll make your answer really <u>stand out</u>.

Exhibit A

Make sure you stick to the question — it's easy to go off the point when you're trying to come up with a really original answer.

Where do topics go to have fun? A theme park...

You'll <u>never</u> get a question that asks you something unexpected, like "Explore how The Tempest suggests that life is all about eating squid". It'll always be a fairly <u>obvious</u> theme, so don't worry.

DIRECTING QUESTIONS

Directing a Scene

The <u>fourth</u> type of exam question you might get asks you to imagine you're a <u>director</u> — the person who's <u>in charge</u> of the performance of the play.

As a Director You Can be Creative

If you get a question on how you'd direct a scene, it's a good opportunity to <u>use your imagination</u>. It's all about how to make the play look and sound great <u>on stage</u>. Here's an example question:

> Act 2 Scene 2 and Act 3 Scene 2
>
> *Imagine you are directing a production of The Tempest.*
>
> **How would you direct the actors playing Caliban, Trinculo and Stephano in these scenes?**
>
> *Explain your ideas with references to the extracts.*

Use the Language and Stage Directions

These questions can be a bit <u>scary</u> if you're struggling to think of good ideas. But there will be plenty of <u>clues</u> in the text which will give you some <u>ideas</u>.

1) <u>Look for LINES that stand out</u>

Find some lines that sound <u>dramatic</u> — happy, angry, scary, anything emotional.

Then think about <u>how</u> the actor should say these lines to really give them <u>impact</u>.

2) <u>Look for STAGE DIRECTIONS</u>

These hint at what's happening on stage — e.g. who's <u>moving</u> where, or what <u>effects</u> (e.g. sounds and lighting) there are.

You can <u>interpret</u> these — say <u>how</u> you'd make them happen.

e.g.

In my opinion, at the stage direction, "*Enter Stephano singing*", he should stagger around from side to side. This would show immediately how drunk he is and start the scene on a comical note.

When Caliban says, "*Do not torment me!*", I would direct him to speak in a shrill voice to show how afraid he is. He could also cower in the corner of the stage to add to this impression.

Quote

What you'd do

Why you'd do it

Quote

What you'd do

Why you'd do it

SPEAK UP!

Die-rector — threatening a clergyman?

As with the other questions, you <u>don't</u> have to come up with loads of really <u>groundbreaking</u> ideas — just give some <u>well-explained suggestions</u> with the odd more detailed point and you're well away.

How the Characters Should Speak

It's fair to say that the <u>most important</u> thing about Shakespeare is the <u>words</u> he uses. So as a director, you have to help the actors get the <u>meaning</u> of these words across to the <u>audience</u>.

Actors Can *Say Their Lines* in Different Ways

1) Have a think about the <u>meaning</u> of the lines, then decide how you can <u>get this across</u> to the <u>audience</u>. It's all to do with <u>tone of voice</u> — e.g. angry, friendly, sarcastic.

2) There's no right or wrong answer. As long as you <u>explain why</u> you think an actor should speak in a certain way, and give some <u>evidence</u> from the play, you <u>can't go wrong</u>.

3) You can even suggest <u>more than one way</u> for the actor to speak a line — the examiner will like this, as it shows you're <u>thinking</u> really hard about the play. Just make sure you give <u>reasons</u> for each suggestion you make.

e.g.

> When Caliban describes to Stephano how to kill Prospero, he could speak the line, "There thou mayst brain him", *in a secretive whisper*. This would show he knows that what he is saying could get him into trouble.
>
> Alternatively, Caliban could <u>speak very clearly and carefully</u>, to show he is working out the plan. As he says the words, "Batter his skull", he could mime the action of attacking Prospero, <u>to emphasise how much he wants to kill him</u>.

Give an idea about <u>how</u> the lines should be said.

Give <u>another opinion</u> if you have one.

Always <u>explain</u> why you have a certain idea. This is the <u>most important</u> part of your answer.

You Can Create a Sense of *Anticipation*

1) <u>Anticipation</u> means wanting to know <u>what will happen next</u>. Shakespeare sometimes creates a feeling of anticipation by letting the <u>audience</u> know something the <u>characters don't</u> — this is called <u>dramatic irony</u>.

What's going on?

Ant is a patient.

e.g.
> Irreparable is the loss, and patience
> Says it is past her cure.
>   Act 5, Scene 1, 140-141

2) Here, <u>Alonso</u> is convinced his son <u>Ferdinand is dead</u>, and says there is <u>nothing</u> that can be done to make things better. But <u>we</u> know Ferdinand is <u>alive and well</u>, and that Prospero is about to reveal him to Alonso.

3) When writing as a director, you can say how you'd <u>add to the suspense</u> of the scene. E.g. For the bit above, you could show Ferdinand and Miranda in the background, behind Alonso's back, as he speaks these lines.

Shtop! Thish play is not ready yet...

Being a director means giving your own <u>interpretation</u> of the play. Keep thinking about the effect you want to create on the <u>audience</u> — they're what it's all about. And be <u>enthusiastic</u> — it works.

DIRECTING QUESTIONS

How the Characters Should Act

The director can also create <u>mood</u> for the <u>audience</u> by thinking about how to get the actors to say their <u>words</u> with a bit of feeling.

Think About How Different Characters Will Act

<u>Different characters</u> will act in different ways. You can <u>compare</u> characters to show how <u>mood</u> is put across to the audience.

(e.g.) *Although Caliban is nervous and excitable, Stephano should appear more sure of himself. When he says, "Monster, I will kill this man", he should talk loudly and confidently, <u>to show he is enjoying taking control of the situation</u>. He could also slur his words drunkenly to add to the comedy.*

Show that you know they <u>don't all feel the same</u>.

Here's your <u>explanation</u> again — really important.

Think about how the characters are <u>feeling</u>, then how to <u>show this</u> in their <u>tone of voice</u>. And remember you can <u>compare</u> different characters and their <u>feelings</u> in the same scene.

Tell the Actors How to Move

They're actors, so make 'em <u>act</u>. Their <u>body language</u> (gestures, posture and movement) has a big effect on how their characters come across, and you can suggest things that aren't in the stage directions. As ever, <u>explain your ideas</u> and stick to the <u>evidence</u> in the play.

(e.g.) *In Act 3 Scene 3, when the banquet first appears, the actor playing Alonso should <u>in my opinion</u> walk slowly up to the food, rubbing his eyes <u>to show that he can hardly believe what has happened</u>. When he says "What were these?", <u>he should turn to the other characters</u> with an amazed look on his face.*

Use phrases like "<u>in my opinion</u>" — they show it's <u>your idea</u> and you're <u>exploring</u> the play.

Describe the <u>effect</u> you're trying to create.

<u>Expand</u> on your idea.

If you're discussing two <u>different ways</u> to direct a scene, try to <u>link</u> your points together.

<u>Linking words</u> are dead useful. They help you move from one part of your answer to the next.

- however
- although
- on the other hand
- in comparison

Get your act together...

So there's <u>a lot to think about</u> in these what-if-you-were-the-director style questions. But they're a really good opportunity to give a good "<u>discussion</u>" — and the <u>more ideas</u> you have, the <u>better</u>.

Appearance & What Characters Do

Directors have loads of <u>other stuff</u> to think about as well as how the actors should say their lines.

Mention What Sound and Lighting You'd Use

1) <u>Sound</u> can be used to create a <u>mood</u>. E.g. In the first scene, as well as the thunder and lightning mentioned in the stage directions, you could add the sounds of <u>waves</u> crashing against the ship and <u>desperate shouts</u> from the mariners, to add to the sense of <u>chaos</u> caused by the storm.

I said "lighting" not "lightning".

DIRECTOR

2) <u>Lighting</u> is also pretty crucial. Again you can add to what's in the stage directions, e.g. when Prospero draws the <u>magic circle</u> in Act 5, Scene 1, the rest of the stage could be <u>dimmed</u>, with just the magic circle lit up in <u>strange, bright colours</u>.

3) Remember to <u>explain</u> every suggestion you make. I know I sound like a broken record saying this, but you <u>absolutely, positively, definitely</u> have to do this. Honestly. I really, really mean it.

Say What Clothes They Should Wear

You can show you understand a scene by talking about the <u>costumes</u> you'd choose for it.

 e.g. When Stephano enters, he would still be wearing his butler's outfit, but it would be torn and dirty because he has been wandering around the island drunkenly since the storm. His clothes could also be covered in wine stains.

You <u>don't</u> have to stick to <u>old-fashioned</u> costumes. Lots of productions today use <u>modern clothes</u> and you can too — as long as you can show how they <u>suit the characters</u>.

Use Loads of Quotes (again)

Just like all the other types of question, you absolutely have to use <u>quotes</u> — but it's actually <u>dead easy</u> to stick a few quotes into these questions. <u>Follow these steps</u> and you're sorted:

I've got it wrong again, haven't I?

- say how you want the actors to speak and act, and what lighting and sounds you'd use

- find a quote that backs your idea up and write it down

- say why you'd do it (you won't get the marks otherwise)

Background music? Sound idea...

Just make sure you're still <u>answering the question</u> — if the question just says "What advice would you give to the actors?", don't go on about the lighting or makeup. But if it just says "How would you direct these scenes?", you can talk about pretty much <u>any aspect</u> of the production.

Revision Summary

So there you have it. Four types of exam question, and oodles of tips to help you with each one. Fair enough, some are easier than others — but you've got to be well prepared for <u>any</u> of those types of question, 'cos you just don't know what'll come up in the exam. And if the sight of the very word "exam" has you breaking out in a cold sweat, it's time to really get learning. Right, enough from me, let's have a butcher's at how much attention you've been paying in this section...

1) If you're writing about a character, is it a good idea or not to give a one-sided description of them?

2) What does "motivation" mean?

3) What should you think about when writing about a character?

   a) The past

   b) The future

   c) Parallel dimensions

4) What does Shakespeare's "use of language" mean?

5) What's another word for mood?

6) What should you do if you get a theme question that seems really complicated?

   a) Read the question carefully and work out the main thing it's asking.

   b) Write a good answer on a different subject.

   c) Give up school and become a cattle rancher in Bolivia.

7) You don't have to use quotes in theme questions. True or false?

8) Name four themes in The Tempest you might be asked about.

9) Explain what is meant by:

   a) anticipation

   b) dramatic irony

10) What does "body language" mean?

11) If you talk about clothes, should they always be old-fashioned costumes?

12) Name three things about a production that the director is in charge of deciding.

13) What do you absolutely, positively have to do every time you make a point in an essay?

   a) Explain the point and give evidence.

   b) Say what lighting you'd use.

   c) Play a fanfare.

TENSION

You could cut the tension with a knife.

The set scenes are the <u>only</u> scenes you need to know in real <u>detail</u>.
Make sure you know these two scenes <u>inside out</u>.

> Ariel reports back to Prospero about his work during the storm. Ariel complains when Prospero gives him more work to do, but Prospero promises to let him go if he helps for another two days.

ACT 1 SCENE 2

Enter ARIEL

hail = *greetings*

be't = *be it*

ARIEL All hail, great master! Grave sir, hail! I come
To answer thy best pleasure — be't to fly, 190
To swim, to dive into the fire, to ride
On the curled clouds. To thy strong bidding task

192-193 *'Give me and all the other spirits your orders.'*
Ariel and all his quality.

193-194 *'Did you organise the storm exactly as I told you to?'*
PROSPERO Hast thou, spirit,
Performed to point the tempest that I bade thee?

to every article = *right down to the last detail*
ARIEL To every article. 195
I boarded the King's ship. Now on the beak,
Now in the waist, the deck, in every cabin,

beak = *front end*   waist = *middle*
I flamed amazement. Sometime I'd divide
And burn in many places — on the topmast,

198-206 *'I made myself look like flames, amazing the crew. Sometimes I split myself up, burning in many places around the ship, then joined myself back together. I was faster than lightning; and the thunder made the waves shake.' Jove was Roman god of the sky, Neptune was god of the sea.*
The yards, and bowsprit, would I flame distinctly, 200
Then meet and join. Jove's lightnings, the precursors
O' the dreadful thunder-claps, more momentary
And sight-outrunning were not; the fire and cracks
Of sulphurous roaring the most mighty Neptune
Seem to besiege, and make his bold waves tremble, 205
Yea, his dread trident shake.

207-208 *'Was anyone brave enough to stand all the racket without going a bit mad?'*
PROSPERO My brave spirit!
Who was so firm, so constant, that this coil
Would not infect his reason?

208-210 *'Everyone went loopy.'*
ARIEL Not a soul
But felt a fever of the mad, and played
Some tricks of desperation. All but mariners 210

brine = *sea*

quit the vessel = *jumped over board*
Plunged in the foaming brine, and quit the vessel,
Then all afire with me. The King's son, Ferdinand,
With hair up-staring (then like reeds, not hair)
Was the first man that leapt, cried 'Hell is empty,
And all the devils are here.'

PROSPERO Why, that's my spirit! 215
But was not this nigh shore?

nigh = *near*
ARIEL Close by, my master.

PROSPERO But are they, Ariel, safe?

ARIEL Not a hair perished,
On their sustaining garments not a blemish,

217-224 'Nobody lost a hair. Their clothes are even cleaner than they were before. I've done what you said and scattered them in little groups around the island. Ferdinand's sitting all alone in a quiet corner, sighing and twisting his arms in knots.'

224-226 'What have you done with the ship and the sailors and the rest of the fleet?'

still-vexed = still troubled by reefs and storms that were dangerous for ships

230-232 'The sailors are below decks. I cast a spell and they're worn out anyway so they're all fast asleep.'

232-237 'The rest of the fleet was scattered but now they've met up again and they're sailing back across the Mediterranean to Naples, all sad because they think the King and his ship are lost.'

charge = task

mid-season = noon

240-241 'It's at least two. We've got to make the most of the time between now and six.'

242-244 'Is there more work to do? Let me remind you that you've made me a promise and you haven't kept it.'

How now = hello

liberty = freedom

I prithee = I pray you, I beg you

or = either

bate me = let me off

252-256 'You do. You think it's a burden to fly across the ocean, run with the wind and go into the warm depths of the earth when the surface is covered in frost.'

But fresher than before, and, as thou bad'st me,
In troops I have dispersed them 'bout the isle.   220
The King's son have I landed by himself,
Whom I left cooling of the air with sighs
In an odd angle of the isle, and sitting,
His arms in this sad knot.

PROSPERO   Of the King's ship,
The mariners, say how thou hast disposed,   225
And all the rest o' th' fleet?

ARIEL   Safely in harbour
Is the King's ship. In the deep nook, where once
Thou called'st me up at midnight to fetch dew
From the still-vexed Bermudas, there she's hid.
The mariners all under hatches stowed,   230
Who, with a charm joined to their suffered labour,
I have left asleep; and for the rest o' th' fleet,
Which I dispersed, they all have met again,
And are upon the Mediterranean float
Bound sadly home for Naples,   235
Supposing that they saw the King's ship wrecked,
And his great person perish.

PROSPERO   Ariel, thy charge
Exactly is performed, but there's more work.
What is the time o' th' day?

ARIEL   Past the mid-season.

PROSPERO   At least two glasses. The time 'twixt six
and now   240
Must by us both be spent most preciously.

ARIEL   Is there more toil? Since thou dost give me pains,
Let me remember thee what thou hast promised,
Which is not yet performed me.

PROSPERO   How now, moody?
What is't thou canst demand?

ARIEL   My liberty.   245

PROSPERO   Before the time be out? No more!

ARIEL   I prithee,
Remember I have done thee worthy service,
Told thee no lies, made no mistakings, served
Without or grudge or grumblings. Thou did promise
To bate me a full year.

PROSPERO   Dost thou forget   250
From what a torment I did free thee?

ARIEL   No.

PROSPERO   Thou dost, and think'st it much to tread the ooze
Of the salt deep,
To run upon the sharp wind of the north,

To do me business in the veins o' th' earth   255
      When it is baked with frost.

ARIEL   I do not, sir.

PROSPERO   Thou liest, malignant thing. Hast thou forgot
      The foul witch Sycorax, who with age and envy
      Was grown into a hoop? Hast thou forgot her?

ARIEL   No, sir.

PROSPERO   Thou hast. Where was she born? Speak!
                                                  Tell me. 260

ARIEL   Sir, in Algiers.

PROSPERO   O, was she so? I must
      Once in a month recount what thou hast been,
      Which thou forget'st. This damned witch Sycorax,
      For mischiefs manifold, and sorceries terrible
      To enter human hearing, from Algiers   265
      Thou know'st was banished. For one thing she did
      They would not take her life. Is not this true?

ARIEL   Ay, sir.

PROSPERO   This blue-eyed hag was hither brought with
                                                  child,

      And here was left by the sailors. Thou, my slave,
      As thou report'st thyself, wast then her servant;   270
      And, for thou wast a spirit too delicate
      To act her earthy and abhorred commands,
      Refusing her grand hests, she did confine thee,
      By help of her more potent ministers,
      And in her most unmitigable rage,   275
      Into a cloven pine, within which rift
      Imprisoned, thou didst painfully remain
      A dozen years, within which space she died,
      And left thee there, where thou didst vent thy groans
      As fast as mill-wheels strike. Then was this island — 280
      Save for the son that she did litter here,
      A freckled whelp, hag-born — not honoured with
      A human shape.

ARIEL   Yes, Caliban her son.

PROSPERO   Dull thing, I say so — he, that Caliban
      Whom now I keep in service. Thou best know'st   285
      What torment I did find thee in. Thy groans
      Did make wolves howl, and penetrate the breasts
      Of ever-angry bears. It was a torment
      To lay upon the damned, which Sycorax
      Could not again undo. It was mine art,   290
      When I arrived and heard thee, that made gape
      The pine, and let thee out.

ARIEL   I thank thee, master.

malignant = *poisonous*

257-259 'Have you forgotten the horrid witch Sycorax, who was so twisted that her body was shaped like a hoop?'

261-267 'I have to remind you every month what you used to be, as you keep forgetting. Sycorax was thrown out of Algiers for all the wicked, unspeakable things she'd done. For some reason they wouldn't kill her.'

with child = *pregnant*

271-283 'Because you couldn't carry out her nasty orders, she got into a terrible rage, and with the help of some powerful spirits, trapped you in a pine tree. You stayed there for twelve years and in that time she died and left you there, groaning away. There wasn't one other person here then, except her deformed child.'

unmitigable = *uncontrollable*

Dull = *stupid*

in service = *as my servant*

288-292 'It was the kind of punishment damned souls get in hell and Sycorax couldn't undo her spell. It was my skills that got you out of the pine tree.'

52

293-294 *'If you complain again I'll rip open an oak tree and trap you inside its woody guts'*

correspondent = *obedient*

299 *'I'll set you free.'*

301-304 *'Go and disguise yourself like a sea fairy. Make yourself invisible to everyone except you and me. Go and disguise yourself then come back.'*

diligence = *care*

Ariel's new disguise

Heaviness = *sleepiness*

Yields = *gives*

310-313 *'We can't do without him. He makes the fire, fetches the wood in, and does other useful tasks.'*

earth = *stupid lump*

within = *inside*

like a water-nymph = *Ariel has changed shape*

318 *'Listen to this.'*

got = *fathered*

dam = *mother*

come forth = *come out*

PROSPERO   If thou more murmur'st, I will rend an oak
And peg thee in his knotty entrails, till
Thou hast howled away twelve winters.

ARIEL   Pardon, master.   295
I will be correspondent to command,
And do my spriting gently.

PROSPERO   Do so, and after two days
I will discharge thee.

ARIEL   That's my noble master!
What shall I do? Say what. What shall I do?   300

PROSPERO   Go make thyself like a nymph o' the sea.
Be subject to no sight but thine and mine, invisible
To every eyeball else. Go take this shape,
And hither come in 't. Go! Hence with diligence!

Exit ARIEL

Awake, dear heart, awake! Thou hast slept well.   305
Awake.

MIRANDA   The strangeness of your story put
Heaviness in me.

PROSPERO   Shake it off. Come on,
We'll visit Caliban, my slave, who never
Yields us kind answer.

MIRANDA   'Tis a villain, sir,
I do not love to look on.

PROSPERO   But as 'tis,   310
We cannot miss him: he does make our fire,
Fetch in our wood, and serves in offices
That profit us. What ho! Slave! Caliban!
Thou earth, thou! Speak.

CALIBAN *(within)*   There's wood enough within.

PROSPERO   Come forth, I say. There's other business
for thee. 315

Come, thou tortoise! When?

Enter ARIEL *like a water-nymph*

Fine apparition! My quaint Ariel,
Hark in thine ear.   *(Whispers)*

ARIEL   My lord, it shall be done.

Exit

PROSPERO   Thou poisonous slave, got by the devil himself
Upon thy wicked dam, come forth!   320

Section 7 — The Set Scenes

ACT 5 SCENE 1
Before Prospero's cell

Enter PROSPERO *in his magic robes, and* ARIEL

PROSPERO   Now does my project gather to a head.
　My charms crack not, my spirits obey, and time
　Goes upright with his carriage. How's the day?

ARIEL   On the sixth hour, at which time, my lord,
　You said our work should cease.

PROSPERO 　　　　　　　　　　I did say so,　　　5
　When first I raised the tempest. Say, my spirit,
　How fares the King and's followers?

ARIEL 　　　　　　　　　　　　Confined together
　In the same fashion as you gave in charge,
　Just as you left them — all prisoners, sir,
　In the line-grove which weather-fends your cell.　　10
　They cannot budge till your release. The King,
　His brother, and yours, abide all three distracted,
　And the remainder mourning over them,
　Brimful of sorrow and dismay, but chiefly
　Him you termed, sir, 'the good old lord, Gonzalo'.　　15
　His tears run down his beard, like winter's drops
　From eaves of reeds. Your charm so strongly works 'em
　That if you now beheld them, your affections
　Would become tender.

PROSPERO 　　　　　Dost thou think so, spirit?

ARIEL   Mine would, sir, were I human.

PROSPERO 　　　　　　　　　　And mine shall.　　20
　Hast thou, which art but air, a touch, a feeling
　Of their afflictions, and shall not myself,
　One of their kind, that relish all as sharply,
　Passion as they, be kindlier moved than thou art?
　Though with their high wrongs I am struck to the quick, 25
　Yet with my nobler reason 'gainst my fury
　Do I take part. The rarer action is
　In virtue than in vengeance. They being penitent,
　The sole drift of my purpose doth extend
　Not a frown further. Go release them, Ariel.　　30
　My charms I'll break, their senses I'll restore,
　And they shall be themselves.

ARIEL 　　　　　　　　　　I'll fetch them, sir.

Exit

PROSPERO   *(drawing a magic circle on the ground)*
　Ye elves of hills, brooks, standing lakes, and groves;
　And ye that on the sands with printless foot
　Do chase the ebbing Neptune, and do fly him　　35

Prospero casts a final spell
on his enemies before
forgiving them.

*1-3 'The different parts of my plan
are all about to come together.
The magic's working, the spirits
are behaving and everything's on
schedule. What's the time?'*

*7 'How are the king and his
followers doing?'*

*7-10 'They're all being held just as
you ordered, like the last time you
saw them — trapped in the wood
which shelters your cave.'*

line-grove =
small wood
of lime trees

*12 'are still
all a bit mad'*

*17-19 'Your magic's having such
a strong effect on them that if
you saw them now it would make
you feel really sorry for them.'*

*21-30 'You're made of air, and you
feel sorry for them, so I should be
even more touched. The things
they've done to me really upset me
but I'll control my anger with
reason. Forgiveness is more
worthy than revenge. If they're
sorry for what they've done now I
don't need to be cross any more.'*

penitent = *regretful, sorry*

*34 'You who are so light you don't
even leave footprints on the sand'*

ebbing = *flowing back with the tide*

Neptune = *god of the sea*

54

green sour ringlets = *dark rings of grass at the base of a toadstool, supposedly made by dancing fairies*

solemn curfew = *nine o'clock bell, beginning of night*

You go.
No, you.

40-48 *'With your help — though you're only weak spirits — I have darkened the sun at noon, called up the winds, and created war between the green sea and blue heavens. I have made storms, and split Jupiter's holy oak with his own thunderbolt. I have made the ground shake and ripped trees up by the roots.'*

50-57 *'Now I'm giving up this violent magic. I'll just conjure up some music — there it is — to soothe Alonso, Sebastian and Antonio, and that's it. I'll break my magic stick and bury it deep in the earth, and sink my books deep in the ocean.'*

plummet = *plumbline, the weight on a string used to measure the depth of the sea*

And for madam... The boiled brains?

air = *tune*

unsettled fancy = *disturbed mind*

63-64 *'my eyes feel sorry for yours and they're crying in sympathy'*

64-68 *'The spell's wearing off. Just as morning takes over from night, their wits are chasing away the confusion from their minds.'*

68-71 *'Gonzalo, you saved my life and you've been a loyal servant to Alonso! I'll make sure you're rewarded in word and action.'*

71-74 *'You treated me and my daughter terribly, Alonso. Your brother helped you — you're suffering for it now, Sebastian.'*

When he comes back; you demi-puppets that
By moonshine do the green sour ringlets make,
Whereof the ewe not bites; and you whose pastime
Is to make midnight mushrooms, that rejoice
To hear the solemn curfew; by whose aid — 40
Weak masters though ye be — I have bedimmed
The noontide sun, called forth the mutinous winds,
And 'twixt the green sea and the azured vault
Set roaring war. To the dread rattling thunder
Have I given fire, and rifted Jove's stout oak 45
With his own bolt. The strong-based promontory
Have I made shake, and by the spurs plucked up
The pine and cedar. Graves at my command
Have waked their sleepers, oped, and let 'em forth,
By my so potent art. But this rough magic 50
I here abjure, and, when I have required
Some heavenly music — which even now I do —
To work mine end upon their senses that
This airy charm is for, I'll break my staff,
Bury it certain fathoms in the earth, 55
And deeper than did ever plummet sound
I'll drown my book.

Solemn music. Here enters ARIEL *before, then*
ALONSO, *with a frantic gesture, attended by* GONZALO,
SEBASTIAN *and* ANTONIO *in like manner, attended by*
ADRIAN *and* FRANCISCO. *They all enter the circle
which* PROSPERO *had made, and there stand charmed,
which* PROSPERO *observing, speaks:*

A solemn air, and the best comforter
To an unsettled fancy, cure thy brains,
Now useless, boiled within thy skull. There stand, 60
For you are spell-stopped.
Holy Gonzalo, honourable man,
Mine eyes, ev'n sociable to the show of thine,
Fall fellowly drops. The charm dissolves apace,
And as the morning steals upon the night, 65
Melting the darkness, so their rising senses
Begin to chase the ignorant fumes that mantle
Their clearer reason. O good Gonzalo,
My true preserver, and a loyal sir
To him thou follow'st! I will pay thy graces 70
Home both in word and deed. Most cruelly
Didst thou, Alonso, use me and my daughter.
Thy brother was a furtherer in the act.
Thou art pinched for't now, Sebastian! Flesh and blood,
You, brother mine, that entertained ambition, 75
Expelled remorse and nature, whom, with Sebastian —

Whose inward pinches therefore are most strong —
Would here have killed your king, I do forgive thee,
Unnatural though thou art. Their understanding
Begins to swell, and the approaching tide   80
Will shortly fill the reasonable shore
That now lies foul and muddy. Not one of them
That yet looks on me, or would know me. Ariel,
Fetch me the hat and rapier in my cell.

Exit ARIEL and returns immediately

I will discase me, and myself present   85
As I was sometime Milan. Quickly, spirit!
Thou shalt ere long be free.

ARIEL *(sings and helps to attire him)*
Where the bee sucks, there suck I.
In a cowslip's bell I lie.
There I couch when owls do cry.   90
On the bat's back I do fly
After summer merrily.
Merrily, merrily shall I live now
Under the blossom that hangs on the bough.

PROSPERO Why, that's my dainty Ariel! I shall miss thee; 95
But yet thou shalt have freedom. So, so, so.
To the King's ship, invisible as thou art.
There shalt thou find the mariners asleep
Under the hatches. The master and the boatswain
Being awake, enforce them to this place,   100
And presently, I prithee.

ARIEL I drink the air before me, and return
Or ere your pulse twice beat.

Exit

GONZALO All torment, trouble, wonder and amazement,
Inhabits here. Some heavenly power guide us   105
Out of this fearful country!

PROSPERO   Behold, sir King,
The wronged Duke of Milan, Prospero.
For more assurance that a living prince
Does now speak to thee, I embrace thy body,
And to thee and thy company I bid   110
A hearty welcome.

ALONSO   Whether thou be'st he or no,
Or some enchanted trifle to abuse me,
As late I have been, I not know. Thy pulse
Beats, as of flesh and blood, and, since I saw thee,
Th' affliction of my mind amends, with which,   115
I fear, a madness held me. This must crave —
An if this be at all — a most strange story.

74-79 'You, Antonio, my own brother, you ignored your conscience and the natural order, and were prepared, with Sebastian, to kill your King. I forgive you, even though you've gone against nature.'

80-82 'Soon they'll totally understand what's happening, instead of being confused.'

rapier = *sword*

85-86 'I'll get changed into the kind of thing I wore when I was Duke of Milan.'

ere = *before*

cowslip = *primrose*

Under the hatches = *below decks*

99-101 'When you've woken the master and boatswain, bring them here, and quickly please.'

Behold = *look*

108-109 'I'll hug you to prove I'm real'

111-113 'I don't know whether you're really him or another magic trick.'

114-116 'since I've seen you the sickness in my mind has lifted. I think it was making me mad.'

116-120 'There must be a strange explanation for this. Have your dukedom back and pardon me. How come you're still alive and living here?'

120-122 'First, let me hug my worthy old friend Gonzalo.'

123-125 'You're still under the influence of the magic of the island so you can't be sure of anything.'

126-129 'I could get you two into serious trouble with Alonso and prove you're traitors if I felt like it. But I won't do it now.'

129 'The devil's speaking through him — it's not true.'

130-134 'As for you, it disgusts me to even call you brother, but I forgive you. Now give me my dukedom back — you've got to.'

rankest = most disgusting

Go on, ask to be Duke again.

Thy dukedom I resign, and do entreat
Thou pardon me my wrongs. But how should Prospero
Be living and be here?
PROSPERO *(To* GONZALO*)* First, noble friend,   120
Let me embrace thine age, whose honour cannot
Be measured or confined.
GONZALO   Whether this be
Or be not, I'll not swear.
PROSPERO   You do yet taste
Some subtleties o' th' isle, that will not let you
Believe things certain. Welcome, my friends all!   125
(Aside to SEBASTIAN *and* ANTONIO*)*
But you, my brace of lords, were I so minded,
I here could pluck his Highness' frown upon you,
And justify you traitors — at this time
I will tell no tales.
SEBASTIAN *(Aside)* The devil speaks in him.
PROSPERO   No.
For you, most wicked sir, whom to call brother   130
Would even infect my mouth, I do forgive
Thy rankest fault — all of them — and require
My dukedom of thee, which perforce I know
Thou must restore.

Index

Index